MENSA®

TOTAL GENIUS
& PERSONALITY TESTS

This 2010 edition published by Metro Books, by arrangement with Carlton Books Ltd.

"Mensa" and the Mensa Logo (globe atop table design) have been registered in the U.S. Patent and Trademark Office by American Mensa, Ltd., and are used by the publisher with American Mensa's permission. Related Mensa organizations own registrations for the mark and logo in other countries.

Metro Books
122 Fifth Avenue
New York, NY 10011

ISBN: 978-1-4351-1739-6

Printed and bound in Singapore

10 9 8 7 6 5 4 3 2 1

MENSA® ᛗ ®

TOTAL GENIUS
& PERSONALITY TESTS

YOUR COMPLETE GUIDE TO GENIUS, INCLUDING PERSONALITY TESTS, KNOWLEDGE TESTS, INTELLIGENCE TESTS AND MORE

Philip Carter
Ken Russell

METRO BOOKS
NEW YORK

American Mensa® Ltd

®

American Mensa Ltd is an organization for individuals who have one common trait: an IQ in the top 2% of the nation. Over 57,000 current members have found out how smart they are. This leaves room for an additional 6 million members in America alone. You may be one of them.

Looking for intellectual stimulation?
If you enjoy mental exercise, you'll find lots of good "workout programs" in the *Mensa Bulletin*, our national magazine. Voice your opinion in one of the newsletters published by each of our 134 local chapters. Learn from the many books and publications that are available to you as a member.

Looking for social interaction?
Are you a "people person," or would you like to meet other people with whom you feel comfortable? Then come to our local meetings, parties, and get-togethers. Participate in our lectures and debates. Attend our regional events and national gatherings. There's something happening on the Mensa calendar almost daily. So, you have lots of opportunities to meet people, exchange ideas, and make interesting new friends.

Looking for others who share your special interest?
Whether yours is as common as crossword puzzles or as esoteric as Egyptology, there's a Mensa Special Interest Group (SIG) for it.

Take the challenge. Find out how smart you really are. Contact American Mensa Ltd today and ask for a free brochure. We enjoy adding new members and ideas to our high-IQ organization. For more information about American Mensa: www.us.mensa.org, or

American Mensa Ltd
1229 Corporate Drive West
Arlington, TX 76006-6103

Email: nationaloffice@americanmensa.org
Voicemail: 800/66/MENSA
Phone: 817/607/0060
Fax: 817/649/5232

A NOTE

Now, before you have read anything about genius, I want you to fill out the form below. You need to list your 10 greatest geniuses of all time together with your reasons for including them. **Don't read the book until you have done this.** Once you have completed your list, go ahead and see what I have to say about genius and discover whether it changes your views or not.

Name   **Claim to genius**   **Reason for inclusion in list**

ANOTHER NOTE

Having decided who your favourite geniuses are, try to ask as many friends and colleagues as possible to tell you the people they consider to be the top geniuses of all time. Make a list below of the people they recommend. I did this and the results, which are discussed later in the book, were fascinating.

Name   **Claim to genius**   **Reason for inclusion in list**

CONTENTS

GENIUS

First, a confession. Reading this book will not turn you into a modern Shakespeare, a latter-day Mozart or the second Einstein. Sorry. The aim of the book is to examine what genius actually is, what acclaimed geniuses of the past were like, and whether it is possible for us to emulate them or, at the very least, to expand our own powers significantly. It is fashionable in certain psychological circles to claim that we all have amazing powers which, if only they could be unlocked, would astonish those who know us. This might be true. It's the unlocking that proves to be the problem.

Do not despair, the book includes exercises designed to unlock whatever you've got by way of creative powers. If you have it, we'll help you find it. We will also be testing factors such as concentration, perseverance, originality of thought and powers of logical deduction. Then we'll go beneath the surface and explore your unconscious! But not yet.

First it might be interesting to examine what people through the ages have considered to be the marks of genius. After all, it is a subject that provokes fierce disagreement. Ask people for a list of their favourite geniuses and you will incite a lot of argument and very little concensus. We have actually done this, and the results of the exercise are reported later. We will consider the lives and work of a number of acclaimed geniuses, and also of some people who are tipped to be geniuses of the future but whose fate still hangs in the balance (one very strong claim to genius seems to be that you should be dead). Would you, for example, give your genius vote to any of the following: Bob Dylan, Sir Clive Sinclair, Michael Caine, Terry Pratchett, Bill Gates, Mervyn Peake, Paul Simon? I bet that made you think, didn't it?

Having got some feel for what a genius is like, we will then look at various factors connected with the genius personality. Intelligence is an obvious one. Is genius really just the same as being very intelligent? If so, why is it that we are not swamped with geniuses? Why is every member of Mensa not acclaimed as the new Goethe or the Michelangelo of the new millennium? How would, say, Mozart have come out of an IQ test? This is an important part of our investigation and I have obtained the help of Robert Allen, former head of Mensa Psychometrics, who has worked closely with highly intelligent adults and children for a decade and probably knows more about them and their behaviour than anyone else in the world. We also help you to examine your own level of intelligence and decide whether it is in the genius category.

However, other factors are almost certainly at work. We will be looking at a range of issues such as perseverance, concentration, originality and topicality (in other words, you might only be a genius if your ideas are produced at the right time).

OBSESSION

William James

A genius is the man in whom you are least likely to find the power of attending to anything insipid or distasteful in itself. He breaks his engagements, leaves his letters unanswered, neglects his family duties incorrigibly, because he is powerless to turn his attention down and back from those more interesting trains of imagery with which his genius constantly occupies his mind.

Talks to Teachers

Now we come to look at the factors which make up the genius personality. My own favourite is Obsession. The one thing which seems to be true of all geniuses is that they were totally obsessed with whatever it was they became known for. We hear of no nine-to-five geniuses. It is common to hear that people of genius were so involved with what they did that they devoted their entire lives to it. They frequently sacrificed love, relationships, family, friends, their health and material comfort, even their very lives, for the subject of their obsession. Some of them may have ended up rich and famous, but many ended poor and despised (take Mozart, for example, who ended his life in poverty and notoriety and was buried in a pauper's grave).

No one who seems seriously worthy of the name genius seems to have considered that his or her chosen path was just a cute career move. In every case I have come across, the element of complete obsession is present. These people all did what they did because they had no other choice. It was what they lived for. When you devote absolutely everything you have to one activity, it stands to reason you might expect to be pretty good at it. Certainly you will rise above the levels of the mere dilettante or plausible careerist. When every hour of every day, and probably your dreams also, are given over to one activity which has you in a grip of steel, you must excel at it.

It is not certain that obsession is enough on its own, though. There are many cases of people obsessed who have simply not had enough talent or who, unhappily, have chosen to plough a barren field, in other words who have invested their all in projects that were misconceived and could never succeed. Also there are people who, though they may have

Georges Louis Leclerc de Buffon (1707 – 1788)

Genius is nothing but a greater aptitude for patience.

Attributed

the dedication, do not in the end have enough ability to rise above the average. My good friend Dr Sam Chaplin works as an archaeologist. His whole life is devoted to the study of the ancient Near East and he will talk for hours about pottery, bones and the corroded remains of bronze weapons. He's fascinating on his subject but, it must be said, can only be tolerated in small doses by those with no deep interest in archaeology. I can manage an hour or so and then I've had enough. However, Sam would be the first to admit that he will never be a *great* archaeologist. He has the right level of obsession but, eventually, it has to be admitted that he has never made a huge impact on the subject as a whole. Also, and this is an interesting point, is archaeology capable of easily breeding geniuses? It is a subject that requires meticulous attention to detail and some high-grade detective work but it is very much the province of worthy drudgery rather than heady inspirations. Who can remember a really great archaeologist?

However, I think obsession is a very good place to start looking for genius. It will remove at one stroke all those who practice the boring art of effortless superiority. Lots of people are

'good at' things. They have a 'good at' mentality which allows them to beat others with little effort and then relax comfy in the knowledge that they are The Best. The most glaring difference between these people and the obsessed ones is that they don't care for their endeavours for their own sake. They have no interest in pushing the boundaries of what they do to the absolute limits. They do not strain every nerve, sinew and muscle to reach heights that they had previously thought unattainable. They just enjoy the rich rewards given to those with flair.

When Beethoven went deaf, he didn't just give up writing music; he sawed the legs off his piano and used the floor as a sounding board so that he could go on making music. He had nothing to prove, he could have sat back and enjoyed the reputation and the money, but obsession means that he was in it for the sake of the music, not the material frills.

Here is another point that we will come back to. Geniuses are often not entirely sane. Some, like Nietzsche, went completely mad and were sent to asylums. Others behaved so oddly as to attract unfavourable notice. If they were lucky, allowance was made for their genius. If not, they often suffered the penalties of popular disapproval. Jean Genet, the French author, led a life of petty crime, homosexuality (strictly illegal at the time) and dissolute behaviour which earned him a lengthy sentence in prison. Eventually the French government decided to let him out on the grounds of his literary genius. Later commentators have noted wryly that, had he been British or American, he would have been lucky not to be

Abigail Adams
(1744 – 1818)

These are times in which a genius would wish to live. It is not in the still calm of life, or in the repose of a pacific station, that great characters are formed... Great necessities call out great virtues.

From a letter to John Quincy Adams,
January 19, 1780

imprisoned because of his genius.

The oddness of the genius personality cannot be entirely attributed to obsession, but that is certainly a very great part of it. When you focus so intensely on one sphere of activity it is frequently difficult, and sometimes impossible, to take account of the feelings and sensibilities of 'normal' people. Also it is quite easy to see how someone who is that obsessed would feel that the petty quotidian concerns of the rest of humanity were not worth considering. Can you imagine, for example, the mind of, say, Michelangelo at work on the ceiling of the Sistine Chapel? How much room would there be left for worrying about everyday matters? Would he remember to pay the rent, buy groceries, or put the cat out at night? Can you conceive of a great genius who did any of these normal, humdrum things?

Listen to Nietzsche: *"I teach you the superman. Man is something to be overcome. What have you done to overcome him?"* and *"The superman is the meaning of the Earth. Let your will say: the superman SHALL BE the meaning of the Earth!"* These are hardly the words of an average citizen. They are obsessive, dangerous, full of inspiration. Nietzsche saw a vision of a world transformed from the petty futility which fills most of our lives. Just before we leave this point let's take one more quotation from Nietzsche: *"He who fights with monsters should look to it that he himself does not become a monster. And when you gaze into the abyss, take care that the abyss does not gaze into you."* I hope that this makes it quite clear that the language of genius is that of obsession. This is a person who lives his ideas with his whole being. He does not merely toy with some interesting concepts and scribble the odd newspaper article to make some money and increase his reputation. He thinks dangerously.

Johann Wolfgang von Goethe
(1749 – 1832)

First and last, what is demanded of genius is love of truth.

Proverbs in Prose

VISION

Another attribute of genius is vision – the capacity to see something which is not apparent to other people. This something may be an idea, a scientific theory, a work of art, anything in fact which the human mind can produce. But it must be new. Any number of talented people can improve endlessly upon received ideas. Often the improvements are extremely impressive. Look, for example, at the improvements in rocket science since von Braun's early efforts with the V-2. Could he have foreseen inter-planetary travel? We now regularly send space vehicles to other planets and are seriously contemplating manned missions. None of this would have seemed a practical possibility fifty years ago. Yet none of it requires much vision. People have very quickly made the imaginative leap from powered flight to rockets to space flight. As often happens, science fiction got the jump on science facts by many years. The vision was tied up in von Braun's original idea. The bit of genius was to work out that you could propel an unmanned weapon over a very large distance. Before that, the Chinese has used rockets, but they were unguided and worked only over short distances, making them an inappropriate starting point for the vision of space travel.

Real genius was also possessed by people such as the Wright brothers who saw the possibility of powered flight even when every sane person knew (not thought but *knew*) it to be impossible. How did they know this? Because the scientists of the time told them so. It had been much thought about and carefully calculated. The best scientific brains of the time knew it would not and could not work. The Wright brothers, however, had a vision. They could see that it could work. They had a very good idea of just how it might be made to work and they were not going to be deterred until they got it right.

The strength of their vision can hardly be overstated. Even when their first experiments succeeded, they were told that what they were attempting was impossible. Their early flights took place in a field beside a railway line. People passing by on trains saw the machine fly. Even so the Wright brothers were openly referred to as charlatans, crooks, or plain madmen. In order to combat that degree of prejudice, they needed to have an unshakeable vision of what they could achieve.

Let's take a jump backwards to Leonardo da Vinci. His problem was not so much public prejudice as plain ignorance. He was dealing in ideas that were not simply new, they were unimaginable to people of his time. He sketched, amongst many other things, a flying machine and a submarine.

The point is that vision differs subtly from originality. Of course, genius produces original ideas, and originality will be an important part of our argument, but I think that what is extraordinary about genius is the way in which it can actually *see* something that does not yet exist except as an idea.

This faculty is perhaps most obvious to ordinary people when they consider works of art. The clarity of vision needed to produce any of the great works of art is of a completely different order from that which most of us enjoy. What's more, more than one artist has spoken not of creating a work of art but of *discovering* it. Great sculpture has been described as chipping off the excess stone to reveal the statue hidden inside. This is a truly remarkable idea. Think for a moment of a statue. Let's take something really well-known like Donatello's David. Can you imagine starting that with the whole statue already visible in your mind's eye? Yet that has to be how it was done. It is equally hard to contemplate Donatello fiddling away with his chisel until he got something he liked.

If you write, as I do, you will know that sometimes the words come in a thin trickle but, when you're really working well, they pour out with no effort at all. However, some people can do better than that. They can see the whole book as a finished entity and just pour it onto the page. The British children's writer Enid Blyton was like that. Now, I'm not proposing Ms Blyton as a genius. She was a poor stylist and her work has frequently been criticized (though its abiding popularity suggests that her ghost may have the last laugh.) However, she was able to write 10,000 words a day and finish a novel within a week! She just wrote, she did not revise. Unkind critics would say that her work was trite and predictable and anyone could dash off such

stuff without much effort. But then critics don't know much about writing, which is why they're critics. Ten thousand words is a great deal of writing to get through in a day. I feel pleased if I've done 2,000 that I'm happy with. You could only write that amount if you could see where you were going, if you had vision.

Take another quite different example. Let's look at Einstein. Even now, most people have difficulty understanding relativity. After all the talk of rubber sheets and weights, it is still just very hard to get your head round some of his concepts. And that's when they're second hand! It's also after many other scientists and science writers have spent a huge amount of effort trying to present Einstein's ideas in an easily understandable form. Imagine what it must be like to have such ideas for the first time! The sheer mind-bending act of vision required to contemplate curved space, for example, is more than breath-taking. Even now, I can write the words 'curved space' but I haven't in my mind's eye the faintest idea of what they might mean. And I don't suppose that I'm very unusual. I think many people have come to accept Einstein as a genius simply by force of custom. He has now been admitted to the Holy Order. But they cannot begin to grasp what he was talking about.

I think we need to consider vision one of the most important attributes of genius. It provides the genius with the focus for all his efforts and abilities. It shows him where and how to apply his intellect. It gives him a place to work out his obsession. It makes perseverance worthwhile. Without vision, genius cannot exist.

THE TEST OF TIME

One attribute of genius is the way in which it stands the test of time. An idea or work of art may seem inspired, brilliant and brimming with originality now, and then be discarded as out of fashion in a few years' time. To be sure of genius we have to look at it from the perspective of history. There can for example be no doubt about Archimedes, Euclid, Plato, Leonardo Da Vinci, Michelangelo, Goethe, or Chopin. They all speak to us clearly from the mists of history. We can look at their works and appreciate them just as much as people did in their own day. Sometimes even more so. The idea of genius as being dependent on the ability to survive over time is not at all new. To illustrate this, look at what Samuel Johnson said about Shakespeare:

The Poet, of whose works I have undertaken the revision, may now begin to assume the dignity of an ancient, and claim the privilege of established fame and prescriptive veneration. He has long outlived his century, the term commonly fixed as the test of literary merit. Whatever advantages he might once derive from personal allusions, local customs, or temporary opinions, have for many years been lost; and every topic of merriment or motive or sorrow, which the modes of artificial life afforded him, now only obscure the scenes which they once illuminated. The effects of favour and competition are at an end; the tradition of his friendships and enmities has perished; his works support no opinion with arguments, nor supply any faction with invectives; they can neither indulge vanity nor gratify malignity, but are read without any other reason but the desire of pleasure, and are therefore praised only as pleasure is obtained; yet, thus unassisted by interest or passion, they have passed through variations of taste and changes of manners, and, as they devoted from one generation to another, have received new honours at every transmission.

Dr Johnson's Preface to Shakespeare (1765)

So, the first thing that Johnson tells us is that a literary giant must 'outlive his century'. It would be foolhardy to argue with Johnson. And, if we are to adopt an arbitrary figure, one hundred years seems a good round one. After all, it is also the period usually quoted after which bric-a-brac becomes 'antique'. So let's consider that a real genius must still have something to say after 100 years has elapsed. Certainly that will remove all those distracting elements Johnson mentions. But it does give us some problems.

What, for example, of Einstein? For modern people, Einstein is probably *the* genius. When I asked friends and colleagues to list their Greatest Geniuses of All Time, he was on every list and usually near the top. But Einstein died only in 1955. He knew (apparently quite intimately) Marilyn Monroe. Here we have a modern man of flesh and blood who existed well within living memory. Can we be certain he was a genius?

I think what gives us confidence in Einstein's genius is how he revolutionized our vision and understanding of the universe. Even if we do not fully understand what he said, we get the strongest feeling that nothing will ever be the same again. Also, of course, in modern times communications are so much quicker that we can have the judgement of the world's scientific community without delay. In Newton's day, it must have taken years for his peers in other countries to assimilate and comment upon his ideas. Now a new theory can be passed around the globe in a very short time. A genius will be subjected to the scrutiny of people throughout the world and, if his ideas can stand up to criticism, he will receive acclaim quickly. In the past such judgements often took until after the individual was dead.

Mozart suffered in this way from posthumous acclaim after living obscurity. He was hailed in his early life as a musician of great talent, perhaps even genius. But then he fell out of fashion and eventually became utterly disregarded. He died miserably never knowing that posterity would regard him as one of the greatest composers of all time.

To return for a moment to Shakespeare, he was not regarded as a genius in his own lifetime either. Certainly he had success, but he also had fierce critics who, from jealousy or perhaps from more noble reasons, were willing to find fault with his work. His status after his death rose gradually. By the 19th century he was utterly unassailable and even literary giants like Samuel Taylor Coleridge regarded him as a god-like being quite beyond the bounds of normal literary criticism. There was even a period in theatre history when his words were spoken in a strange, artificial way that sounded nothing like normal speech. Apparently, dramatists at the time thought Shakespeare was *far* too grand to be made to sound realistic.

Modern communications have changed the way we look at celebrity. Now, instead of reputations spreading slowly by word of mouth, it is possible for someone to be known all around the globe in seconds. There is therefore a very obvious trend to instant celebrity. This has had a knock-on effect in the realms of genius. At one time a reputation would have grown slowly and painstakingly.

16

Ezra Pound
(1885 – 1972)

*Ezra Pound
(1885 – 1972)*

Genius [...] is the capacity to see ten things where the ordinary man sees one, and where the man of talent sees two or three, plus the ability to register that multiple perception in the material of his art.

Jefferson and/or Mussolini, 1935

People would have taken years, even centuries to evaluate the contribution an individual had made. Many people went to their deaths quite unaware of the awe in which they would be held by succeeding generations. Now things are different. Because people get known quickly, they are also subject to the snap judgements of their peers around the world. The accolade of genius is handed out much more freely than before.

Democracy has also crept into the process. In former times only the wealthy, powerful and well-educated would have had access to information. The man in the street was certainly unaware of Newton or his theories, had never heard Mozart's music, had never seen one of Canaletto's paintings. These were all experienced and judged by a tiny elite. Now all the information anyone could possibly want or even think of is flashed around the globe nearly instantaneously by television, radio, newspapers, magazines and the internet. That means that everyone can join in the fun pastime of making judgements about who is, or is not, a genius.

Thus the title of genius is now thrust upon the shoulders of those who are certainly successful and talented, but whose achievements have not even begun to be tested by time. Let's look at a couple of examples. When I questioned people about their favourite geniuses, the most popular modern name was Bob Dylan. Whether Dylan is or is not a genius is not the point; we're merely concerned here with his longevity in the genius stakes. Dylan was born in 1941 which means that, at the time of writing, he isn't even a pensioner! He came to general notice when introduced to the public by Joan Baez in the Sixties. In the following 30 years, his fame has gone right round the world. Having said that, how long will the fame last? Even now it is clear that Dylan's real appeal is to the generation that discovered him. Talk to a bunch of fifty-somethings (not to say sixty-somethings) and you will find Dylan fans aplenty. Most kids have never heard of him. Does this mean that he will end up forgotten as his generation fades away?

All modern musicians have an advantage that was denied their predecessors. Their work is recorded. It will remain available *as they performed it* for inspection in centuries to come. Dylan's fans say that a huge part of his appeal comes from his actual performance and that, without hearing the man, you cannot appreciate what he was. Certainly this is borne out by some dire performances from his imitators. Listen, if you can bring yourself to do it, to certain tribute bands and other pop artists turning Dylan songs into mush, and you will see what I mean.

Geniuses of the past were denied the opportunity of having their artistic performances captured for posterity. We can have no idea of exactly how Beethoven played. Even paintings, which have often been carefully preserved for posterity, are so time-worn as to be quite different from the originals. Art critics and restorers argue fiercely about the merits of restoration which, however skilful, can give us only an approximate idea of how the original looked.

To quote Paul Williams' excellent biography of Dylan:

Paul Williams:

For individuals to have access to as much different work by one contemporary performer as is available to you and me in the case of Dylan is something new under the sun, suggesting whole new possible realms in the relationship between artist and audience. The documentation of performed art via sound recordings and film/video also makes possible a kind of immortality for performed art that before this century was available to the work of composers and playwrights but not to singers, musicians, or actors. Now performances as well as compositions are able to endure across time.

Dylan

In future the test of time will still apply but the rules will have changed subtly. Work will still have to be good enough to seem important to future generations but, in addition to the content of the work, the *style* can also be considered. This may seem trivial but, as Williams said of Dylan, much of his genius lies in his style and in the relationship between artist and audience. If that were lost, it might be harder for future generations to see what the fuss was about.

In addition to this factor, now that public opinion has created a certain 'star' element in the judgement of genius, the fact that the actual person can still be examined long after he or she is dead will be of the greatest importance. Hawking, for example, has a presence that comes directly from his illness. The sight of the tortured body which contains a mind that can only communicate by means of a synthesized voice has turned him into an icon that will still be recognized by future generations. In a sense his ideas, important though they are, have been overtaken by the public perception of him as a genius and it is that perception, rather than the merits of his theories, that will ensure his continuing place as a genius in the history of science.

John Dryden
(1631 – 1700)

Genius must be born, and never taught.

Epistle to Congreve, 1693

INSPIRATION

Genius has much to do with popular acclaim. In the past this would have been the acclaim awarded by one's intellectual peers and maybe also that given by the rich and powerful. Today, with the democratization of information, acclaim has to be awarded by the public, both nationally and internationally. Without acclaim there can be no genius or, at least, if it does exist, it will be wasted because its products will go unnoticed. In order to earn this acclaim, the genius must be able to inspire his public. This was hard enough in earlier times when, at the very least, the public consisted of fellow experts who would mostly have been well informed about his field of endeavour. Even then there was no guarantee that they would accept revolutionary ideas, in fact it was quite likely that they would not. Look at the sheer incredulity that greeted Pasteur when he informed his fellow scientists that we share our world with uncountable millions of micro-organisms. Surely that couldn't be true? If they were all floating around in the air, how could we see through them?

The position now is even stranger. The genius must receive acclaim from people who know nothing at all about his subject. This can produce strange effects. Take the case of Stephen Hawking and *A Brief History of Time*. The book has become a best-seller and Hawking is popularly believed to be a genius. Yet it is well known that most people who buy the book never manage to read it and that many people who subscribe to his genius do not even try to understand his ideas. The truth is that Hawking *seems* to have the stuff of which genius is made. Firstly there is his known brilliance as a young man. There are plenty of people still around who remember his early days and vouch for his enormous intellect. Then there is the tragedy of his devastating illness. Most people would have died of Motor Neurone Disease years ago. Hawking, confined to a wheelchair and able to write by moving only one finger, strikes a chord with everyone. Surely a man who overcomes such huge difficulties and squeezes out words incomprehensible to the common man *must* be a genius. Finally, there is his synthesized voice which gives him the air of a computer that has lived its life in California. There is a slightly eerie, but by no means unpleasant, quality to the voice. Thus Hawking is hugged to the popular breast as a man of genius. And this is by no means meant to cast a slur on his achievements. He is undoubtedly a man of huge courage, tenacity and intellect (and yes, I did read the book). However, only time will tell whether anything he has written will be of long-term value or whether it will eventually be superseded by other theories and then quietly forgotten.

The notion of genius as a sort of popularity contest is a strange one. Why should people with no qualifications be allowed to judge someone who has spent his whole life struggling with great philosophical problems, sublime works of art or abstruse scientific theories? The answer is Inspiration. We look to geniuses to inspire us, to lift us out of our normal existence and give us a feeling that there is more to life than making a living. This leads us to two paths which, though separate, are connected. One is the path of intellect (in which, for this purpose, I will include the achievements of art). Some people appreciate genius for the sake of its products. Every day, many people throughout the world are deeply moved by great art, literature and music. Concert halls are filled, opera houses are busy, people flock to art galleries, books are sold by the million. The works of genius continue, often centuries after they were created, to influence our lives and to offer us inspiration in a variety of forms.

Consider Shakespeare. His works are difficult to understand even for those with some background in English literature and history. Yet in many ways he inspires not only his own nation but others as well. It is fascinating to note that the German edition of his plays is regarded as not just a competent translation, but a literary work in its own right. And, of course, every year hundreds of books, articles, educational videos and even films appear which are directly drawing their inspiration from his work.

The effect Shakespeare had on his native language is also enormous. Many of the things he wrote were so greatly liked that they entered the language and are now quoted, often unconsciously, every day. He also gave the British-speaking peoples a sense of history and of the greatness of their past. People who would never dream of going to see a Shakespeare play regard him as a national treasure beyond price. People even see their history through his eyes. It is well known that much of what Shakespeare presented as historical fact was made up to please his audience and especially powerful people who might be, or might become, patrons. The most scandalous example of this is his treatment of Richard III, who was sent limping down through history with a hunch back and an evil disposition that he may well not have owned during his life. However, so great was Shakespeare's authority that now nothing can be said that will ever really erase the impression he made.

It is doubtful whether many geniuses have given thought to their role as inspirers of their fellow men. Many of them lived in times when it was doubtful whether their works would be seen by more than a relatively few people. It is certainly true that Shakespeare would have been shocked beyond belief to discover that his fame had spread around a world and he was known not only in countries that he had never heard of, but in places which were not even countries in his day. However, whether it was the intention of the genius to inspire or not, it is that inspiration which becomes a very powerful force in deciding whether the genius gets the recognition he deserves.

This says something strange about society. In many societies intellect is distrusted, even despised. Yet it is also admired by those who do not understand what it is achieving!

MAD, BAD AND DANGEROUS TO KNOW

Edward Robert Bulwer-Lytton, Earl of Lytton
(1831 – 1891)

Genius does what it must, and talent does what it can.

Last Words of a Sensitive Second-Rate Poet

Seneca has told us, '*There is no great genius without some touch of madness*'. But was he right? If so, then genius is a heavy burden and not something anyone would actively seek. The evidence, however, is not strong. A quick flick through our genius file (leaving aside, for the moment, our discussion about who is and is not a genius and simply accepting popular opinion) should serve to convince us: Shakespeare, Einstein, Beethoven, Goethe, Leonardo, Mozart, Hawking, Feynman, Byron, Peake, were all perfectly sane – even if sometimes a trifle odd. Of course you can think of mad geniuses. We have mentioned Nieztsche elsewhere and Van Gogh also springs to mind as someone whose hold on sanity was tenuous. There have been occasional instances where genius and insanity went hand in hand, but the correlation is very far from being significant. So is that all we need say? Was Seneca simply wrong?

I think that it is interesting that Seneca, a man of great intellect himself, should make such a remark. Also his words are clearly reflected in the attitudes of the general public. There is a great distrust even of common-or-garden intelligence and much more so of genius. The truth is that people on the whole do not like to be made to think and do not, in particular, like people who make them think or who show signs of excessive intellectual activity in themselves. Expressions such as 'egg-head' and 'smart Alec' are thrown routinely at anyone who shows signs of intellectual endeavour. The Sun newspaper, that bastion of enlightened popular opinion, reserves the label 'beardie weirdie' for those with a penchant for facial hair. And is it pure coincidence that beards are more popular in intellectual circles? Almost certainly not.

What is it about thought that makes people uncomfortable? It's hard to know where to start. The main problem is that, if you think about life quite hard, it raises some very disturbing questions. For example, the

Buddhist view that we are born to age, sicken and die, though unattractive, is pretty much the truth. This is not, it is important to say, by any means all that Buddhism has to say on the subject. Most of us have had such thoughts from time to time, especially when we feel depressed. However, there exists something like a thin, transparent protective layer over most minds. It stops us from thinking morbid thoughts. It allows us to ignore our mortality and comfort ourselves with the reassuringly trivial. We say things like, 'I've too much to do to worry about all that,' or 'It doesn't do to think too much,' or (if you're British) 'Let's have a nice cup of tea.'

There are countries such as France, Germany and Israel, where intellect is recognized and highly valued. However, even here it is only a small percentage of the population who are prepared to meet the deepest questions of life head on. And there are very good reasons for this. If you consider life carefully you have to consider the question: What is it for? If you do not accept any of the pre-packaged religious answers, then you have

a philosophical problem on your hands. If your life is taken up with wondering about the purpose of existence, it may mar your ability to carry out the myriad of trivial daily tasks necessary to survival. A nation of philosophers would almost certainly be an idle and indecisive bunch. Practical tasks demand practical thinking and decisive action, and only a small percentage of the population can be spared for speculative thinking.

In the past we have had the Church and universities as a safe haven for those who want to think. Society has, in its own way, recognized that we need such people and has made room for them. But it has built a fence around them to avoid them infecting the others. Professors are, by popular consent, always considered eccentric (and many of them, by common standards, are). Of course, clerics have always had a rather ambivalent reputation. On the one hand they have been thought wise and holy, but on the other there has always been a deep suspicion towards them. However, anyone *outside* these safe havens who shows signs of excessive thought is

Alan Alda
(b. 1936)

Be as smart as you can, but remember that it is always better to be wise than to be smart

> *Samuel Butler*
> *(1835 – 1902)*
>
> *Genius [...] has been defined as a supreme capacity for taking trouble [...] It might be more fitly described as a supreme capcity for getting its possessors into pains of all kinds and keeping them therein so long as the genius remains*
>
> *Notebooks, Genius, 1912*

really playing a dangerous game. Writers, for example, are frequently ignored if they say anything that challenges the established order or, if they push it too far, they may be silenced. In some countries this will happen by the crude methods of persecution and in others by the less obvious application of commercial pressure or social disapproval.

Take the case of Salman Rushdie. Leaving aside arguments about the literary merit of *The Satanic Verses*, it is significant that he was persecuted simply for thinking dangerous thoughts. It is also interesting that the profoundly anti-intellectual public has little difficulty in recognizing dangerous thoughts even when it doesn't fully understand them. It is well known that many of the people who burnt Rushdie's book had never read it. How could they? It was far too dangerous for that!

Back to genius. There are other attributes of genius that we have looked at elsewhere which add to the popular impression of near-insanity. Geniuses, as we have seen, are frequently obsessive. Most of us are content to live our lives in low gear. We distract ourselves with trivia, gossip, take up hobbies, make a snack, drink coffee and work because we get paid for it. Our mental life has all the intensity of a candle flame. The genius, on the other hand, is like a searchlight. He can direct all his energy, which by ordinary standards is already formidable, with laser-like intensity to one all-important task. On the other hand he probably forgets what he regards as trivial matters because they would take up much-needed mental capacity. This makes the genius an uncomfortable person to live with. He is probably not much good at personal relations because he never has time to practise and, in any case, he may not find them important. Many geniuses are on record as treating their families badly, not through wanton cruelty so much as through pure neglect.

There are other facets of genius that may be mistaken for madness. Vision is an example. People with vision do, by definition, see things differently from the rest of us. They see possibilities where others see none. They see answers where the common herd are not even aware of the question. Think, for example, of the famous story of Archimedes in his bath. According to legend, when he noticed the way his body displaced water in the bath he instantly worked out the principle of specific gravity. He was so excited that he leapt from the bath and ran naked down the street shouting, 'Eureka!' (I have it). Did his neighbours glance over to each other and say to themselves, 'That Archimedes is quite some physicist'? Or did they say, 'That loony old man at number 32 has *really* lost it this time!'?

> *Elizabeth Barrett Browning*
> *(1806 – 1861)*
>
> *Since when was genius found respectable?*
>
> *Aurora Leigh, bk VI, 1857*

I leave it to you to guess.

I think that our attitude to intelligence, let alone genius, must change. It is appalling that almost the last minority one can discriminate against with impunity is those of high IQ. This happens everywhere, but it is particularly upsetting when it happens to kids. In schools it is still quite common for bright kids to be called rude names, often by the teachers. Say 'moron' or 'loser' and you'd be looking for a new job (and possibly a new place to live). Call a kid 'egg head' though and the world laughs with you. Teachers who wish to hide their dislike behind a mask of concern use the tactic of treating intelligence as though it were the symptom of an illness. It is amazing that some doctors and psychologists will go along with this. The Mensa Foundation for Gifted Children is constantly receiving calls from mothers who say things like, 'They say my child is a nuisance in class. The doctor/psychologist says it's Attention Deficit Hyperactive Disorder. They want to give her Ritalin.' They come up with even more bizarre labels like 'borderline autistic' for a child who is lively, communicative and interested in a wide variety of subjects which, unfortunately, the teacher doesn't understand.

There are, fortunately, wonderful exceptions. In Wales the Brynmawr School in Gwent and St Joseph's in Newport both started projects to help gifted pupils. The initiative spread and others such as Pershore High School and Kings' School, Canterbury have joined in. Maybe, just maybe, we will eventually arrive at a stage where people are not suspicious of high intelligence but are willing to treat it as another human attribute, and one that is of value when nurtured and handled with respect.

> *Sir Max Beerbohm*
> *(1872 – 1956)*
>
> *I have known of no man of genius who had not to pay, in some affliction or defect either physical or spiritual, for what the gods had given him.*

IS HIGH IQ THE SAME AS GENIUS ?

Robert Allen has worked with highly intelligent people in Mensa for 10 years. In addition, as CEO of the Mensa Foundation for Gifted Children, he has been involved with exceptionally intelligent children and the problems surrounding their education. He is therefore one of the most qualified people in the world to comment on high IQ.

JF *Can you start by explaining a little about IQ and how it is measured?*

RA There have been a large number of IQ tests developed over the years but they all attempt to measure the same thing, what is called 'fluid' intelligence.

JF *What exactly is fluid intelligence?*

RA It is, if you like, the raw material of intellect. As far as possible it shouldn't be dependent on education. Ideally, it should be a measure of pure brain power.

JF *How is that done?*

RA It isn't at all easy. We know that there are a couple of skills that correlate highly with intelligence. One is the ability to work with numbers and the other is verbal dexterity. However, both are, to quite a large extent, dependent on education. The other problem that arises is that testing these abilities can be unfair to candidates who are from another culture. For example, it isn't fair to judge someone's verbal ability when they are being tested in a language that is not their own. Even so, such tests are frequently used as part of IQ assessment just because they do demonstrate intelligence so well. But if you want to get at IQ divorced from learning, you need to use what are called Culture Fair tests. These usually depend on spatial relationships.

JF *How does that work?*

RA Let's take Raven's Matrices as an example. The candidate is presented with a series of diagrams a bit like pieces of wallpaper. Each one has a swatch missing and underneath there are six possible swatches which might complete the pattern. However, only one of these is the logical answer. As the test continues, the logic required to work out the right answer becomes increasingly complicated.

JF *So what exactly is a 'high IQ'?*

RA Although these tests all use different scales, they measure the same thing, just like Celsius and Fahrenheit give different numbers for the same temperature. However, on all tests the average is 100. The vast bulk of the population is to be found at this point. Then something interesting happens. The numbers fall away quite evenly on either side of the average. It's sometimes called the Bell Curve because it looks a bit like the cross section of a bell. It means that there are the same number of highly intelligent people in the population as there are people who are severely mentally subnormal.

JF *And what do you regard as 'highly intelligent'?*

RA Well, when I worked for Mensa we accepted for membership people in the top 2% on any recognized test. But, of course, that's an arbitrary figure. Someone who falls outside that band may still be very bright.

JF *So would you call those people in the top 2% geniuses?*

RA God no! Absolutely not.

JF *Why not?*

RA IQ is really about processing information. It measures your ability to assimilate information very quickly and then work out how to make use of it. That might be an ability that is of use to a genius but it is by no means essential and certainly having that ability does not mean you can do other things well.

JF *Are you saying that highly intelligent people are not necessarily able in other ways?*

RA Of course. It's a bit like an engine. It may be very powerful but unless it's linked to something it just spins uselessly. I know a lot of people like that. Being told that they're highly intelligent produces a rush of blood to the head, but it never occurs to them to ask what they're going to do with that ability. Worse still, people sometimes think that because they score highly in an IQ test they can do *anything* if only they choose to put their mind to it. Unhappily this proves not to be true.

JF *Have you met anyone of genius in Mensa?*

RA No.

JF *Some people call Sir Clive Sinclair a genius.*

RA Clive had the idea that computers should be of use to everybody, not just scientists and businessmen. That was quite visionary but it was not his idea alone. In Britain he is regarded with a mixture of respect and amusement. He has had some very good ideas and some spectacularly bad ones. I don't think his reputation will survive him.

JF *So do you think that high IQ and genius are unconnected?*

RA No, there is a connection but not a simple one. I think that all geniuses must have been highly intelligent but by no means are all highly intelligent people geniuses. There are just so many other qualities that go to make up genius. Many of them are to do with character rather than intellect. You can be very bright but lack the qualities of character that make you effective in what you do. In fact I would say that this is the main problem of highly intelligent people: they tend to lack the will to achieve.

JF *Why do you think that is?*

RA Because they are so very good at seeing through things. They can always find faults with what other people do and, which is worse, they can find faults with what they do themselves. This affects them in a variety of ways. Some get disheartened and want to do nothing. I've met lots of intellectual drop-outs who just fritter away their time because they cannot believe enough in anything to apply themselves.

You also get people who will indeed apply themselves, but in a very nasty destructive kind of way. They spend their whole lives criticizing under the impression that they will make things better that way. One man said to me, "I'm the grit in the machine. If I foul it up enough someone will take the whole damn thing to bits and give it a good oiling. Then we'll have a better machine." It didn't work, of course. People just wrote him down as a pain in the behind and ignored him. A lot of them get involved in very nasty, twisty games playing. Once you start to use your intellect destructively, you can do yourself and those around you huge amounts of damage.

Then you get the people who decide to devote themselves to some eccentric interest. It can be anything from the occult to World Government. They feel safe because there is no outside point of reference. There is no real standard by which you can judge success. I had lengthy correspondence, mainly one-sided because he needed no encouragement, with a man who believed that there was a conspiracy to introduce Single World Government. He wasn't mad or even paranoid, just too clever for his own good. He had taken a plausible theory – we haven't room to go into it – and allowed his intellect to work it up into a whole way of life. A less intelligent person would have used common-sense to see that it was all a house of cards.

JF *Is there any field, apart from academic research, in which high intelligence is really useful?*

RA *Properly applied*, high IQ is always useful. The problem is that these people have great trouble in finding reasons to apply themselves. The great exception, of course, is the huge growth in the IT industry. Bright people have completely taken over IT.

JF *What's wrong with that? The whole world runs on computers now.*

RA Nothing is wrong with it at all. The growth of IT is an incredible phenomenon. At no time in human history have so many intellects, from so many nations, been focused on one field of endeavour at the same time. And IT itself has made this concentration of effort possible. The problem, if you can call it a problem, is that people can lose themselves in it. The whole subject is huge and, as more is discovered, it gets bigger all the time. Each time you answer a question you get a dozen more. Each discovery opens up new vistas of things yet to be discovered. It's all hugely exciting. It's often the salvation of highly intelligent people, especially some of the kids. It's the first thing they've come across that really absorbs them and gives them a feeling of purpose.

JF *So what's your point?*

RA I think IT provides bright people with an opportunity to display a number of the attributes that you associate with genius. They do become obsessed, they do develop huge powers of concentration, they do have enormous vision when they consider the possibilities, they do have original thoughts, and certainly the effects of what they are doing will be with us for hundreds of years to come.

JF *So will IT produce a great clutch of geniuses?*

RA Ah, *that's* what makes it so interesting! Have you read 'Metaman'? The author points out that humanity is starting to act like one superorganism. We are able to concentrate our efforts so that huge intellectual and material resources are directed to solving a problem. And that is what is happening with IT. In fact it is largely happening *because* of IT. What we are getting is the coming not of a clutch of human geniuses but one supergenius. In the future, the whole concept of genius, at least in certain areas, may become collective rather than individual. I cannot imagine that works of art or literature would benefit from the same treatment.

JF *You've done a lot of work with gifted kids. We often hear them called 'genius children' by the media. What are they like?*

RA Gifted kids have a kind of buzz to them. At their best they radiate energy and enthusiasm. And they have *boundless* curiosity. When they are happy about themselves they can be extremely creative. If they've been well treated and well educated, they can be a delight to meet. Unfortunately they quite often aren't happy.

JF *Why not?*

RA Two main reasons. The first is that, just like highly intelligent adults, they suffer from the, 'What is life all about, and is it really worth it?' syndrome. This can be destructive in adults but really devastating in youngsters. The last thing a teenager needs on top of the usual problems of adolescence is a heavy dose of existential angst. The other reason is that teachers are very poor at recognizing really bright children. There is a popular idea that a very high IQ child is just like a normally bright child but more so. People are unwilling to recognize that high IQ children are different in kind rather than in degree. They frequently have no interest in school work, but cultivate exotic interests of their own. They may appear dull in class because they aren't interested. Absolutely dreadful handwriting is almost universal with very bright kids, which is unfortunate when teachers tend to regard neatness as a cardinal virtue. When they do show signs of interest they can ask very awkward, searching questions. Teachers are not usually well equipped to deal with this. They often see it, not as a sign of praiseworthy intellectual enquiry, but as a subversive desire to flout their authority. Very often we see attempts made to 'diagnose' bright children as suffering from any number or medical conditions from dyslexia and dyspraxia to Asperger's Syndrome and Attention Deficite Hyperactive Disorder. Often what they are trying to do is stick a convenient label on the child so that they don't have to deal with the real problem, or the fact that the child is considerably brighter and more versatile than they themselves are.

JF *Are any of the children you know in the genius category?*

RA One of them will quite likely turn into a genius one day. I can think of a couple of 'possibles' but I think that a genius needs to *make* something, whether it be a work of art, a scientific theory, or a piece of music. The kids I know have so far done nothing but show how clever they are. If they go on to apply that cleverness to something, they might qualify for genius status eventually.

JF *Can I ask you for your list of the ten greatest geniuses of all time?*

RA OK. I'll vote for Daruma, Leonardo Da Vinci, Donatello, Shakespeare, Mervyn Peake, Aldous Huxley, Rimsky-Korsakov, Einstein and, as modern geniuses, I'll take a chance on Colin Wilson and Bob Dylan.

JF *You didn't vote for Umberto Eco. You made me spend* hours *reading him and now you're telling me he's not a genius!*

RA I think Eco is very interesting, amazingly widely read, always worth listening to but, at the end of the day, I don't really think anything he says is particularly important. You can put him on *your* list if you want, though.

THE AREAS OF GENIUS

A question we have not yet considered is whether genius can occur in any field of human enterprise or whether it is limited to certain areas. If I look at the list of geniuses contributed by my family, friends and acquaintances, it is obviously a great concentration on fields such as art, music, literature, science, and philosophy. There are some interesting omissions. Why, for example, has nobody included political or military leaders? It is quite common to hear of some politician that he was 'the most brilliant young man of his generation'. So what went wrong? Why did his highly successful career, which often ended with at least a knighthood and maybe a seat in the House of Lords, not entitle him also to the name of genius? It is quite possible that he showed some of the other symptoms we associate with genius. He may well have worked tirelessly, been obsessed with his tasks and even been an inspiration to his nation. Why was the final accolade denied?

Similarly military leaders seems to be disqualified from consideration when genius is being considered. Of course, you hear the phrase 'military genius' used. Rommel was regarded as such a genius. But the title is restricted. It's as if being a military genius is not enough to qualify for the full title. It's a bit like getting a half-blue at Cambridge - a good effort but not the Real Thing. Even someone like Oliver Cromwell, a military genius who went on to rule his nation and found a Parliamentary democracy which was the mother of all other democracies, is not regarded as a genius in the full sense.

I feel that one of the things people look for in genius is a sort of other-worldliness. People who are simply good, or even brilliant, at day-to-day tasks are not regarded as special. They may be called 'genius' in a light-hearted, good-natured sort of way, but it isn't deeply meant. Famous sports stars are often given the title (until the next game in which they make a mistake, at which point it is rapidly withdrawn). Successful businessmen also get loaned the genius name for a short time. But the nature of business is 'what goes up must come down' and success, even if long-lived, is seen by many as being temporary. It's unlikely that anyone will seriously call Bill Gates a genius, or Rupert Murdoch, or any of the other multi-millionaires who inhabit the globe. Also what they do is, let's face it, rather grubby. It does not inspire. Making huge amounts of money may, in some ways, impress. Money gives power, and *that* is impressive to many too. But inspire? No. Money and power are not inspiring.

What is? Is it intellectual endeavour that sets hearts fluttering? After all, many geniuses have been great intellectuals. And yet, if we look at the whole area of intellectual work, we can see that there are great swathes of it which are devoid of genius. That's because much academic work is really high-class clerking. It involves the relentless and painstaking observation of facts, the recording and analyzing of data. But it does not necessarily involve dramatic conclusions. How many archaeologists get to make a splash in the public consciousness? I wondered about Schliemann, the German who discovered the ruins of Troy. He was a brilliant man, he could reputedly learn any language in a matter of weeks, and he managed to prove that what he had discovered *was* Troy when the conventional wisdom of the time held that Troy was only a myth. Yet, when I asked around, few people had even heard of Schliemann and none of them was prepared to give him their genius vote.

There are many academics who labour worthily in fields which seem unwilling to provide the stuff of which genius is made. Now, is it that there are certain areas in which genius simply does not apply, or is it that geniuses are only drawn to certain pursuits which are congenial to their talents? Why do we not hear of genius geographers, historians, social scientists, linguistics experts, economists, palaeontologists, or cartographers? There must be dozens of other fields of effort that have not produced publicly-acclaimed geniuses.

My strong conviction is that genius needs drama and inspiration. There has to be an almost religious awe connected with it. The genius must seem to be in touch with a level of human experience which is of a different order from that which most of us experience. The only example I can think of in which a man engaged in a 'boring' subject became acknowledged as a genius is that of Charles Darwin.

Darwin was a zoologist and botanist. These are subjects that mainly involve observation and careful note-taking. Even other scientists regard them somewhat askance. If you can remember your school days you may have found that biology was regarded as a 'soft' science for people who had not quite got what it takes. However, Darwin proved them wrong. His principle of evolution was so revolutionary that it rocked the whole world, not just the intellectual establishment. Also it was quite simple and although people initially misunderstood him (often on purpose, for it was an unpopular theory), they found themselves touched at a very deep level by what he said. After all, the idea that humans are just a superior sort of ape and not a special effort on the part of the Creator must have come as a bit of a shock.

For a while Darwin was a villain, even a bogeyman. He had threatened what people then saw as one of the foundations of religion and, because society was still nominally religious, he had also attacked the fabric of that society. As time passed his theories became more accepted and once that began to happen they were seen as truly inspiring. The idea that living species evolve is a huge one. Once you manage to untie yourself from the notion of special creation, evolution is a liberating concept. Of course, many religious people were quick to see that the Bible did not have to be taken literally on this point.

Even so, Darwin manages to remain a controversial figure. There are many people who still question his ideas, though more subtly than before. The religious objectors have not yet entirely gone away and, especially in the US, Creation Science has carried on the fight on behalf of special creation. Far from damaging Darwin's status, this has meant that his relevance is no whit less now than it was a hundred years ago.

Genius needs to be relevant. An idea that is surpassed does not have the stuff of genius in it. For example, in spite of the discovery of the strange world of quantum physics, no one has entirely superseded Newton's ideas on gravity. Euclid's geometry is still taught in schools. No one will ever do a better job on the ceiling of the Sistine Chapel than Michelangelo. No one will ever carve a sexier David than Donatello. You can look at any of these works of genius today and see them as entirely up-to-date. They influence your life right now. There is nothing of the museum piece about true genius, it hits you right between the eyes NOW.

Genius also needs to transport us to areas we may not otherwise visit. It cannot take us to familiar places and show us sights we have already seen. Talent may do that, but genius performs a higher function. There is, in a special sense, something religious about true genius. It must fill us with wonder and awe. It need be attached to no particular religion. People have a need for self-transcendence and we use many methods to achieve this. At the most prosaic level we can achieve it with simple things like colour and sound. A pretty picture, a beautiful landscape, even bright colours, are all enough to take us out of ourselves. And of course we use external stimulants. We don't like to say that very much because we pretend to believe it is wrong. But most people use alcohol to achieve a sense of otherness. Television can also be very effective at taking us away. These also can give us a brief escape from drabness. And of course we use each other. Sex is one of the great escapes from drab reality. It is often said that sex is 99% in the head and this is quite true. Sex is one of the most liberating experiences humans enjoy. It is probably the nearest thing we have to real magic. The fact that it is in itself largely imaginary is beside the point. Lord Chesterfield told his son that, 'The pleasure is momentary, the position ridiculous'. Silly man.

Many people would consider religion as the chief means of achieving self-transcendence. For in religion we are united with something far greater than our limited selves. We are attempting to get closer to the Ground of Being. Only some of us find that harder than others. Some people's religion *is* strange, wonderful, visionary, mystical and deeply satisfying. Others just go to church on Sunday. And for many these days religion is just empty. They do not believe in God and cannot for the life of them understand how anyone else could.

Genius, however, brings us close to that state of self-transcendence we all crave. If we cannot achieve it directly, maybe we can get close enough to those who do achieve it that some might rub off on us like fairy dust. The genius can interpret that state for us and make it to some degree accessible. With the work of great artists, musicians and writers, this mystical aspect of their work is quite easily seen. You do not have to be hyper-sensitive to feel the sublime quality of great music, or be deeply moved by a beautiful painting. Scientific theories may take a bit more work. But there is an excitement about science that cannot fail to infect anyone with an interest. It is interesting that Einstein often made religious references in talking about his work. For example:

At any rate, I am convinced that He [God] does not play dice.

Science without religion is lame, religion without science is blind.

You do not have to understand Einstein's work, or that of any other great scientific genius, to get a feeling for the sense of revelation that they receive from their labours. When you are dealing with the very fabric of time and space and trying to understand just how those things work, you must have an overpowering sense of being near to the very source of all knowledge. The experience cannot fail to be powerfully uplifting, and it is not just a matter of intellectual satisfaction, like solving The Times crossword puzzle in record time. It surely has to work at a much more fundamental level than that. Even for people who have a problem with the idea of God, there must be a great sense of the profundity of all existence. That this is important to the genius himself is understandable, but why should it affect the rest of us?

Of course, there are plenty of people around who *do* know what Einstein, Newton, Hawking and others were talking about. For those people, it is not hard to share in the sheer excitement of discovery. The interesting thing is that it rubs off on so many people who have no real idea what it's all about. This may seem risible but I don't think, on reflection, that it is. In former times people looked to saints to provide their contact with the infinite. Ordinary people may have not understood what it was that the saint could see within the holy visions, but they had the greatest faith that they might, in some small way, share a part of it by connection with the physical person of the saint.

I think that in our day we have replaced to some extent the saint with the genius. We feel that by admiring and studying people of such rare abilities we can in some way incorporate their greatness and their ideas into our own lives. Why else has Einstein become such an icon? He was, by any objective standard, a rather strange-looking man – very far from handsome. So why do people want to wear his face on their T-shirts, or decorate their rooms with posters of him? It is because he has come to represent the very idea of a greatness which most of us will never achieve and, by adopting him as a symbol, we feel able to approach just a little nearer to that heightened state of being. This is what we want of genius. We need to have that sense of vision and we only get it from certain areas of human endeavour. Science, yes, the Arts, yes, Philosophy, yes, Music, yes, Literature, yes. Even Architecture or Engineering are sometimes considered to qualify as works of genius. But those who work in disciplines that require endless drudgery but produce in the end nothing that is more than merely useful need not apparently apply for the title of genius.

IS GENIUS INTERNATIONAL ?

> *Robert Schumann*
> *(1810 – 1856)*
>
> *Hats off, gentlemen – a genius!*
>
> *On first hearing Frédéric Chopin's music, 1831*

One of the things I have spent time considering was whether genius had to apply across national boundaries. The thing that strikes you immediately is that all the great geniuses of history are internationally known. However, Einstein was very clear about the fragility of this international recognition. When addressing the Sorbonne in 1929 he said: *"If my theory of relativity is proven correct, Germany will claim me as a German and France will proclaim that I am a citizen of the world. Should my theory prove untrue, France will say that I am a German and Germany will declare that I am a Jew."*

People seem to respond to genius regardless of where it comes from. Of course, there is a pleasant glow of national pride involved in having a home-grown genius but, as far as I can see, it is unusual to deny genius just because it is imported. There are exceptions. For example, both Nazi Germany and the countries of the Communist Bloc refused to recognize genius on ideological grounds. But that was primarily a matter of politics rather than nationality. The Russians had no problems recognizing the greatness of Marx, even though he was a foreigner. The Nazis disapproved of Freud because he was a Jew, but also because his ideas were uncongenial. In this they made common cause with their Communist opponents who also found Freud's views too dangerous to tolerate.

It is interesting just how far genius can cross national boundaries. Shakespeare is a wonderful example. His work is quite inaccessible even to those who speak English. There is so much in Shakespeare that is simply not apparent to people studying his plays several hundred years after his death. English and American children who learn about him at school have to have the plays 'translated' for them. Yet his reputation is just as great with people who have no knowledge of English at all. We have mentioned the famous German

34

William James
(1842 – 1910)

Genius means little more than the faculty of perceiving in an unhabitual way.

The Principles of Psychology, 1890

translation that is regarded as a work of literarture in its own right, but other countries also have translations which ensure that Shakespeare's work is well known by a huge international audience. Of course, there are themes in his plays that are timeless and beyond nationality. The love of Romeo and Juliet, the terrible dilemma that their families' enmity places them in, and the dreadful irony of their death are all completely comprehensible whether the language is English or Urdu. Similarly the dreadful indecisions of Hamlet, the thirst for revenge shackled by the inability to act, are quite clear in any language. And much of what Shakespeare's characters say, once stripped of its antique trappings, still calls out to us clear as any bell. The fine nuances of language that are held up for admiration to an English-speaking audience are not in the end essential for an understanding of the plays.

Of course musicians and artists have a great advantage when their works are taken abroad because they are dealing in media that require no translation. You can understand Rodin's The Kiss whatever language you speak and you can respond to Beethoven's music without

the slightest knowledge of the language and culture from which it sprang. Science also enjoys this advantage since much of it is expressed in the international language of mathematics and is thus immediately comprehensible to other scientists throughout the world.

Are there national geniuses who do not get recognition abroad? It is hard to think of any. Of course, every country has its own heroes whose work has a strong national appeal. However, it seems that when their work is really great it gets known abroad in spite of the difficulties. Burns, that most Scottish of poets, has travelled the globe (admittedly with some help from expatriate Scots). Samuel Beckett did even better and exported himself bodily to France where he added to his reputation as a writer in English by writing with distinction in French.

It seems that you cannot keep genius confined. It has a habit of spreading and being recognized wherever it goes. This is so much the case that we may take it as a defining characteristic of genius: if you aren't known for what you do all around the world, you don't qualify.

Charles Churchill
(1731 – 1764)

Genius is of no country.

The Rosciad, 1761

GENDER AND GENIUS

Now for a touchy subject. Can a woman be a genius? The current socially acceptable attitude is that women can do anything men can do. If you really want to score Brownie points you add the word 'better'. Certainly there has been unprecedented progress made in women's rights over the last century, and much of it has been concentrated into the last 30 years. Attitudes have shifted unimaginably in such a short time. In the 1950s and early 60s most respectable middle class women stayed at home and looked after the house and children. With a few exceptions, women only went out to work in case of financial need, not because they wanted to or because they needed a career for reasons of personal fulfilment. Even when that started to change, there were many areas which were thought of as strictly off limits. Women in the military, for example, were not there to fight but to help out behind the lines. Women in the media were to sit around looking pretty and dealing only with 'women's subjects' like cookery, fashion, and maybe a little light interior decoration. It was said that a woman newscaster was unthinkable because they would be far too emotional - they might cry if they had to announce a major disaster. Of course, you couldn't have women judges, or fire fighters, or managers, or bankers. In fact, if it didn't involve being 'feminine', then women couldn't do it. That situation changed drastically over what, in historical terms, was

the blink of an eye. Now, although the fight for equality is by no means won, it has come a very long way. Certainly any man who now says, 'Women can't do that' is taking a big risk with his personal safety. But it's not just a matter of the pressure created by women themselves. Society's attitudes have changed a lot. People of both sexes would actually find many attitudes which were common 30 years ago personally offensive today.

Where does that leave genius? In my survey I asked numerous friends, colleagues, family members and even complete strangers, to list the ten greatest geniuses of all time. The respondents were from a variety of backgrounds, though mostly well educated. Not one of them mentioned a woman's name. When I started to research the subject, it was noticeable how many writers referred to 'men of genius' and *meant* 'men'. When I drew this to people's attention and ask them whether, on second thoughts, they would vote for a woman, a few people muttered about Marie Curie. But it was clear that their hearts weren't in it. It was just the only name they could lay their tongues to.

Of course, some of the problem is that, in the past, men would have set the agenda as far as genius was concerned just as they did in so many other areas. Women would have been actively discouraged from engaging in fields which were regarded as 'not suitable' for them. Also, even had a woman decided to stick her neck out and go against the prevailing mood, it would have been men who eventually judged her efforts. And the judgement would have been harsh. One of the reasons Joan of Arc ended up at the stake was that her conduct was 'unwomanly' and involved her going around dressed as a man.

We have considered elsewhere the similarity between genius and sainthood and how both give ordinary mortals a chance to contact that which is greater than themselves. The odd thing is that women have always been quite acceptable amongst the saints. Although there have always been the usual male-inspired ideas that women are in some way impure and the purveyors of sin and temptation, nobody has ever thought to maintain that *some* women could not have access to the divine. Female saints abound. So why not female geniuses?

When you look at the fields in which geniuses seem to crop up it is noticeable that they are mainly male dominated. Music has produced many women performers of the greatest talent, but no noted composers. There are many women artists and some sculptors but, again, they are relegated to the ranks of the talented rather than the exalted heights of genius. Women in science are rather harder to find and in mathematics and theoretical physics, which is where geniuses seem to congregate, they are rare as hens' teeth.

This raises the question of why people do not regard the things women do well as areas in which genius can be found. There have been many notable women singers and musicians whose efforts have easily equalled anything men have done. But for some reason performers, however talented, do not seem to qualify except in very rare cases. You could make a very reasonable case for, say, Maria Callas to be regarded as one of the greatest opera singers of all time. Similarly you could insist, with reason, that Margot Fonteyn was one of the world's great ballerinas. But they do not make it onto the genius list.

As we have noted, genius seems to be in the gift of the general public. Unless people believe that you are one, you don't get elected. What they look for in genius seems to be something exclusively male. This is hard to understand but nonetheless true. You would imagine that, given the progress in women's rights that we noted at the beginning of this chapter, that attitudes in the area of genius would also have changed. But I have to reiterate, no one (even friends who are normally hot on women's issues) thought to include a woman in their list. Given the need for genius to have stood the test of time, and the overwhelming sexual oppression of earlier centuries, it seems that the most likely cause is simply that women have not yet had time to accumulate many geniuses – both because of lack of access to the necessary careers, and because of public prejudice. Will Jane Austen, Agatha Christie or Curie be geniuses in fifty years? We'll see!

*Lucius Annaeus Seneca
(4BC – AD65)*

There is no great genius without some touch of madness.

Moral Essays

EVIL GENIUS

Must genius always be beneficial? Can it serve evil? These are important questions which we need to consider. The most obvious subject for our enquiry is Adolf Hitler, Führer of Germany's Third Reich. Was Hitler a genius?

Let's measure him against the check list of genius attributes we have so far established. To start with, Hitler was clearly a man obsessed. Even as a young man he had formulated his plan and followed it, step by step, to its conclusion. If you need evidence of his obsession, you need look no further than the Final Solution in which he planned to solve the Jewish 'problem' by eliminating the entire race. What better evidence of obsession could you have? To follow your beliefs to such a monstrous end must require a mind that is utterly obsessed and quite immune not only to all human feelings of compassion but also to the sheer horror of the task it was about to initiate.

Did Hitler have vision? Certainly he did. Anyone who reads *Mein Kampf* will see that his rise to power, his military conquest, his plan to inflict Nazi ideology on the rest of the world, were all carefully planned well in advance. He was able to see the whole thing spread out before him and, remarkably, his plan was so detailed and accurate that others ignored it as the work of a madman. No one, except his followers, really believed that Hitler would do all the things he had set out so carefully and methodically in his book.

And Hitler had perseverance. He suffered ridicule and imprisonment as the penalty of his early activities. He was by no means some Johnny-come-lately rabble rouser who saw an opportunity and grabbed it quickly. He had to struggle against the German establishment, the weak democracy of the Weimar Republic, the aristocracy, the well-established officer class that ran the military and the newly-ascendant Communist Party. His road to power was a long, hard one which he trod with great fortitude. Not only good men are capable of persevering in the face of difficulties.

What about inspiration? There can be no doubt that Hitler did inspire people. Remember that before his arrival Germany had been in an economic mess. Also the nation was humiliated by its defeat in the First World War and was lacking self-respect and confidence. Hitler gave people back the sense of German's greatness, the belief in themselves, and the idea that they had a mission to go out and bring German culture, under the banner of Nazism, to the rest of the world. Anyone who has seen the newsreels of the Nuremberg rallies will have no difficulty in understanding that here was a man who knew what people wanted and how he could give it to them. He was an inspiration to a nation desperate for hope. What's more, his power was so strong that he continues, long after his death and the destruction of his vile political system, to

> *Thomas Carlyle*
> *(1795 – 1881)*
>
> *Genius (which means the trancendent capacity of taking trouble, first of all)...*
>
> *The Life of Frederick the Great, book IV*

inspire others of like mind. In spite of all that is known of what Hitler was and the evil to which he gave birth, there are still people who find him a compelling figure and who would emulate him if they could. There are others who, though lacking the sick mentality needed to imitate Hitler's deeds, are still under his spell to the extent that they study his life and work. Some of these people are perfectly respectable historians who would not as much as kick a cat in temper. But nonetheless they are arrested by the evil fascination which Hitler managed to engender.

What about the test of time? Can there be any doubt? Will he ever be forgotten? No. His deeds will continue to be recalled with horror for generations. What's more, the effect of those deeds is still with us. And some of those effects are strange. It is arguable that, without the Holocaust, there would have been no modern state of Israel. Much of the impetus towards its creation came from the horror, not to say guilt, other nations felt at what had happened and, in many cases, what could have been done to prevent it from happening. Consider also the European Union which was largely set up to prevent a repetition of the

events of the Second World War. A union of the democracies of Europe is probably the last thing Hitler sought but it is very much part of his legacy – a reaction to his evil genius.

I think on the evidence we have seen we must, with the greatest reluctance, admit that there is such a thing as evil genius and that Hitler is the prime example. It is interesting that elsewhere in this book we have noted that political leaders are not usually credited with the title of genius. In fact we decided that, of all the fields of human endeavour, politics and military leadership were two fields where genius was not found. Therefore it is even stranger that my other candidate for evil genius is also a political leader, Josef Stalin.

Stalin was not the visionary that Hitler was, but then he didn't have to be because he inherited a political philosophy that was ready-made. Communism was already a thriving political force and Stalin (or Dzughashvili to give him his real name) became an enthusiastic supporter but was not one of the intellectual founders of the movement. However, he had persistence. He was expelled from theological college for his views and lived under the assumed name of

Koba whilst constantly on the run from the police. He was arrested, imprisoned and exiled repeatedly.

Stalin was obsessive in his struggle to complete the Communist revolution in the USSR. He had millions of Russians arrested, tried and either executed or sent to the Gulag as political prisoners. His ruthlessness was easily the equal of Hitler's and he was utterly dedicated to his cause. But he also had the power to inspire. A recent TV interview questioned young communists who had volunteered under Stalin's rule to go and build a power station in Siberia. These were now old men and women but, as they told of the heroic efforts they made to complete this task for the good of the Revolution, their eyes glowed with fervour which had not left them in the intervening years. They cheerfully admitted that they had eventually found out what Stalin was really like but that nothing could entirely erase the love they felt for him. Their work on the power station had given them a sense of purpose that few of us ever achieve. It was fascinating to be told by the commentator that the living conditions for the young volunteers were actually as dreadful as those suffered by the political prisoners but, because they were full of the inspiration they had received from Comrade Stalin, they thrived whilst the prisoners died.

I think that, with regret, we have to admit that genius can be evil. It would be nice to pretend that it was not so. We *could* decide that only those who do good could be admitted to our roll of fame. However, to do that would not be honest. It would ignore the fact that some people who are, in human and moral terms, quite repugnant, also have characteristics that make them exceptional. These characteristics are very similar to those we see in the great geniuses and it would be foolish not to acknowledge that fact. The point is that geniuses can be persuasive, charismatic, visionary and so forth. The responsibility falls to us to ensure, before we listen to what they have to say or follow their recommendations, that they are not evil.

Haile Selassi

Throughout history, it has been the inaction of those who could have acted; the indifference of those who should have known better; the silence of the voice of justice when it mattered most; that has made it possible for evil to triumph.

MODERN GENIUS

Who are the geniuses of the present day? This is a tough question. One of the things that we have seen is that genius needs to stand the test of time. Anyone whose reputation is still going strong a hundred years after his death is in with a big chance. That, of course, does not stop people trying to pin the title on favoured contemporaries. In my survey two names in particular came up repeatedly: Bob Dylan and Terry Pratchett. We will examine their claims to the title shortly.

Something that hastens the process of becoming a genius in modern times is the frenetic pace with which information now gets passed around the globe. Like most people these days I'm not only in touch with the rest of the world through news broadcasts, but in personal touch through friends on the internet. I can tell you about a motor crash in Baltimore this morning not because it has been or ever will be on the BBC news, but because an email friend just sent me an eye-witness account. This information revolution means that we don't have to wait long for everyone to have their say on any given subject. At last there really is such a thing as world opinion (or at least an opinion that represents the developed world). This means that any new candidate for the title of genius can be considered and evaluated both by his peers and by the general public in double-quick time.

However, this hasty consideration of genius, though it has its attractions, does have its weaknesses. Some ideas, like Einstein's Theory of Relativity, can be considered by the greatest scientific minds of the age and found to be unassailable. If the theory is spread around the world and no one can find a hole in it then the likelihood is that it will stand up for generations to come and maybe in perpetuity. However, in artistic fields there is far more subjective judgement involved and it is not at all certain that the much-lauded work of today will still excite such universal admiration in some distant tomorrow.

There are far too many contenders for the title of Genius of Our Times for us to consider them all. From the lists that were given to me by friends and colleagues, there are a few names that deserve special mention. Stephen Hawking is an interesting one. Almost everyone thought of him immediately as a genius of today. But why? No one I spoke to had really studied his ideas. Some people had struggled through *A Brief History of Time* but could not summarize the contents or give an explanation of its main ideas. Yet everyone was adamant that Hawking is a genuine genius. As I have said elsewhere, he has become an icon of his age. TV regularly shows his instantly-recognizable tortured body, his strange synthesized voice and, just in case you have missed the point, has him gazing out over the galaxy in a strangely God-like pose. Without wishing to deride his achievement one bit (because I, too, don't understand what he's talking about), I would point out that he is a new breed of genius. A genius by popular consent and without recourse to rational judgement. This is, to say the very least, an extremely interesting development.

Bob Dylan is quite a different case. Many people put him on their list, especially when I asked older friends who first encountered his music in their youth. Robert Allen, of Mensa Psychometrics, told me a good story about Dylan. Apparently in the Sixties you could buy a poster with a picture of Dylan looking moody and super cool. On it was written the phrase: *Do you understand his words?* According to Robert the truthful answer was, 'No'. But, of course, the *implied* answer was, 'Right on, man!'

There is really nothing in Dylan's music that would mark him out as special. His tunes are mainly trite. His words, however, are much more open to discussion. There have been plenty of books trying to analyze Dylan's lyrics, so I won't go into all that here. Let's just say that a significant number of people would vote for Dylan as an important modern poet. The test will come if people still remember him next century. Did he say anything that went deep into the human psyche? Did he plant seeds that will grow into poetic trees? Who can tell? There are also people who will be happy to tell you that his lyrics are pretentious nonsense not worthy of a moment's consideration. Only time will tell.

Then there's Dylan's public persona. People who only remember him since he became famous will see him as that super cool guy who dominated a generation. When interviewed, he frequently spoke in riddles which made a lot of people think that what he said was very profound. Few people realized that when he started out as a kid, Dylan used to tell jokes and fool about on stage. His early act had a large element of comedy in it. Did he discover later on that he had something deep and meaningful to say? Or did he just discover that being a cool dude with a mysterious image was better for business?

I'd *like* to believe in Dylan as a genius. I like his songs and often quote bits from his lyrics. Deep down I have my doubts but, what the heck. Let's just say that the jury is still out on this one.

Another person who regularly gets mentioned as a genius is Terry Pratchett. At first Pterry (as his fans call him, and to know why you need to read his book *Pyramids*) was a purely British taste. As we have seen, people who do not cross national boundaries do not get to be geniuses. Now, the Americans have discovered Pratchett and so have others. He has even been translated into Swedish.

Pratchett writes fantasy. Most of his novels concern the Discworld, a flat planet that moves through space supported on the backs of four elephants who, in turn, stand on the back of Great A' Tuin the star turtle. Within this environment he manages to cover a huge range of material.

It is unusual for a humorist to gain international recognition, because humour differs so much from country to country. It is particularly unusual, though by no means unknown, for something the Brits find funny to amuse the Americans. Brits and Yanks may seem alike superficially, but often prove to be widely different in their tastes or perceptions. So Pratchett's international appeal bodes well for his claim to genius.

Is there more to him than that? Can humour really be a field in which you can find genius? Pratchett points out that just because something is funny, it does not mean that it isn't also serious. His books use the fantasy location of the Discworld to look at religion, philosophy, politics, science and many other issues. A perfectly serious book has just been published by a couple of British scientists (Ian Stewart and Jack Cohen of Warwick University) on *The Science of the Discworld*.

Certainly his supporters are vocal in their defence of his claim to genius. I recently saw a TV documentary about him in which a number of people referred to him as 'the new Dickens'. One lady even went so far as to approach him at a signing session and call him 'the new Shakespeare' to his face. Terry, I noticed, did not put her straight on this point.

My own feeling is that Pratchett is an immensely talented humorous writer. I have read nearly all his books and enjoyed them hugely. Certainly a lot of what he writes is memorable and even thought-provoking. His ceaseless exploration of the nature of magic is much more profound and interesting than you might believe. If your first impulse is to scoff 'But there's no such things as magic!' then you are really missing the point.

Terry shows all the signs of obsession. His output has been huge and the Discworld series alone runs to more than a couple of dozen novels. And he has vision, there's no doubt about that. He can show you things you certainly never thought of before. He also inspires people and has a degree of charisma. In short, he has many of the qualifying signs linked to genius that we have discussed elsewhere in this book.

I think that, like other popular authors (and I'm thinking of people like P.G. Wodehouse, Harper Lee, J.D. Salinger and others who have been taken to the hearts of the people whilst remaining largely despised by the literati), Pratchett will remain popular with people for a long time. As he is only in his early sixties, we may hope that he will be with us in person for many years to come, too. But even after he has gone, I think his reputation will persist. Whether it persists long enough and whether, after mature reflection, his insights are considered deep enough to qualify him as a genius, I don't know.

Heinrich Heine
(1797 – 1856)

No author is a man of genius to his publisher.

Attributed

INTELLIGENCE TESTS

As we have seen elsewhere, genius is not just the same as high IQ. However, there is an undoubted connection between high intelligence and genius. The following tests are intended to give you an idea of the level of your intelligence though, being unstandardized, they cannot give you a true IQ. If you'd like to know what your official IQ is, contact your local Mensa organization and they will fix up a test for you. You will find contact details at the front of this book.

TEST 1
SPATIAL REASONING

Spatial problems are very frequently used as a measure of IQ. There are two main reasons for this. First, this sort of non-verbal reasoning is in no way connected to acquired knowledge. It is not about anything you were taught at school. It therefore comes closest to getting at the real stuff of intelligence. Other tests, such as those of numerical and verbal skill, are also important, but they have the disadvantage that a good education may easily produce someone who scores highly on such tests but whose true IQ is actually being exaggerated by the effect of the previous training. Second, spatial reasoning is immune to the problems inherent in language and is therefore what psychologists call 'culture fair'. In other words, people who may be uncomfortable with a language-based test (young children, for example, or people who are taking the test in a language which is not their own), will not be disadvantaged.

THE TIME LIMIT FOR THIS TEST IS 30 MINUTES

Q1   Which of these is the odd one out?

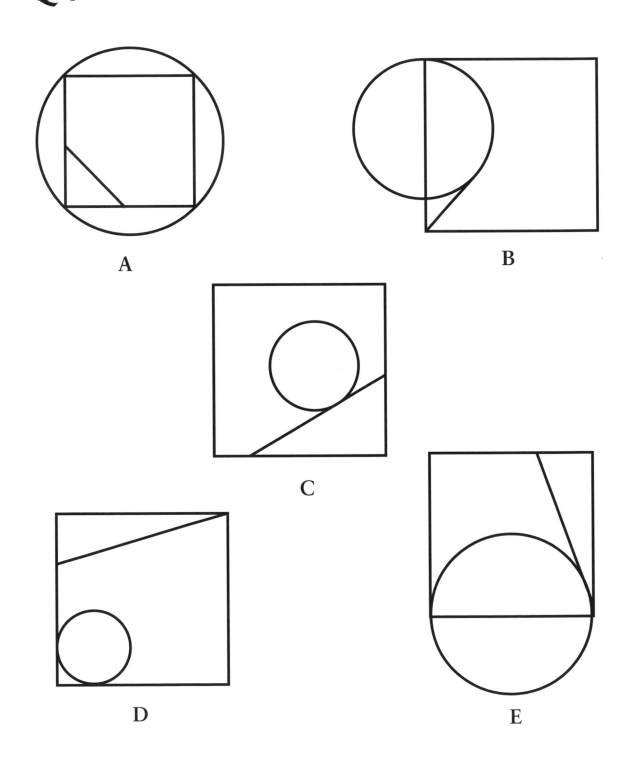

A

B

C

D

E

Q2

What comes next in this sequence: A, B, C, D or E?

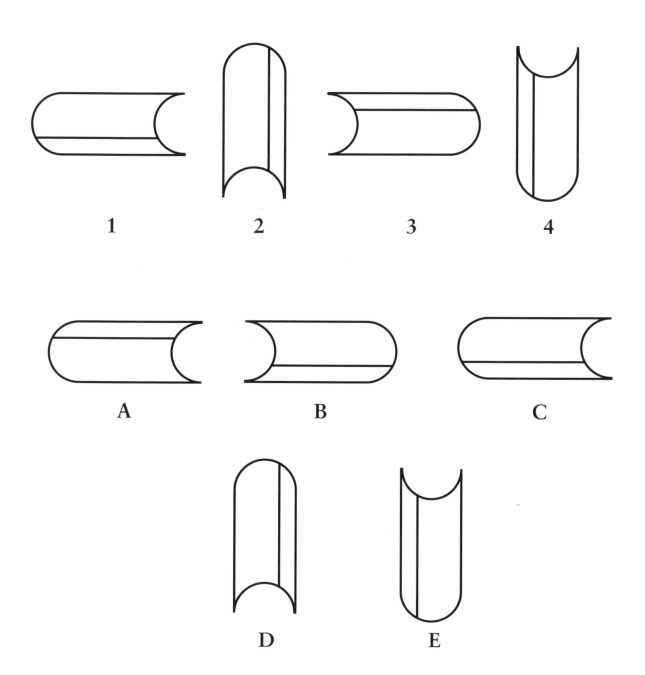

1   2   3   4

A   B   C

D   E

45

Q3 What comes next in this sequence: A, B, C, D or E?

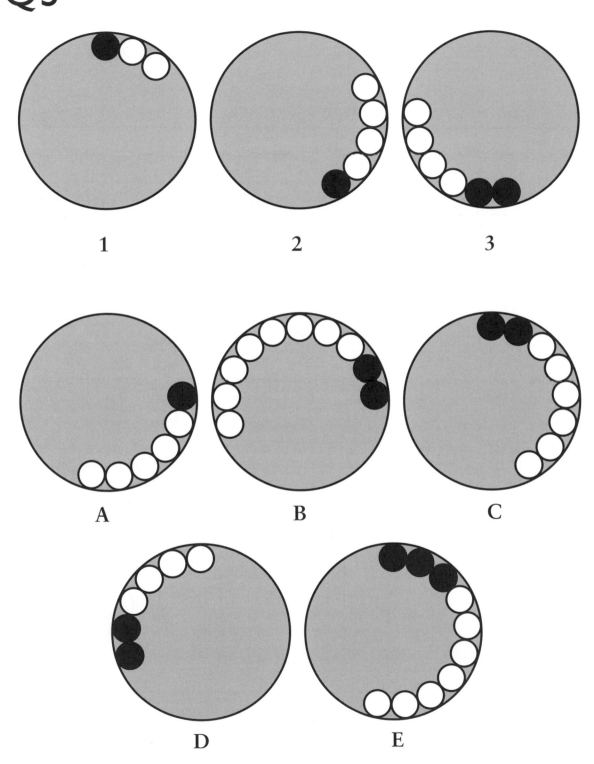

1

2

3

A

B

C

D

E

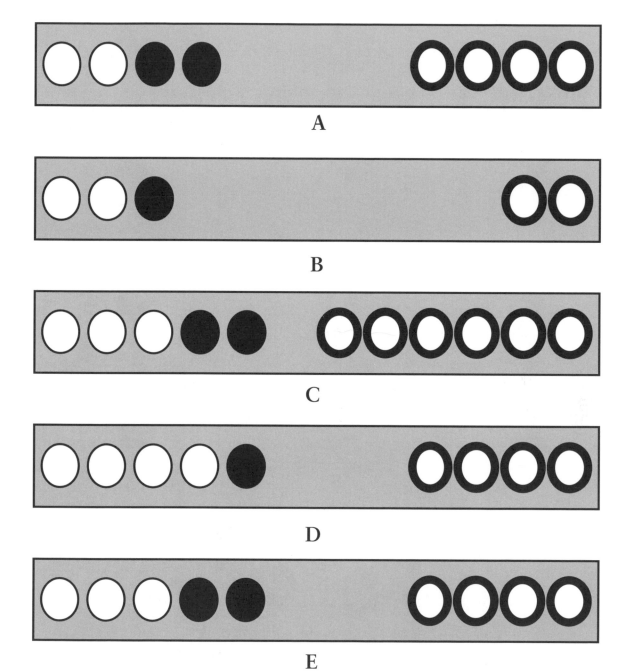

Q4

Which of these is the odd one out?

A

B

C

D

E

Q5

What comes next in this sequence: A, B, C, D or E?

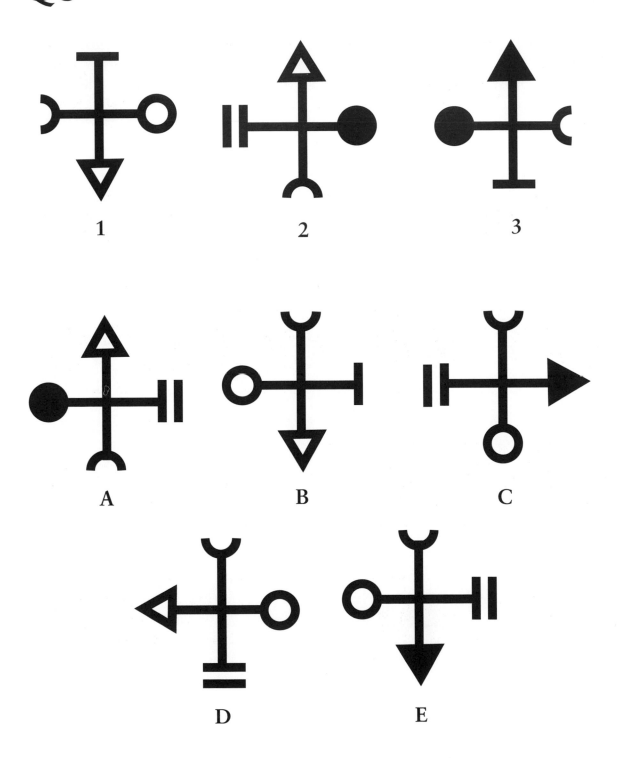

1

2

3

A

B

C

D

E

Q6

Which is the odd one out?

A   N   E

A   B   C

F   H

D   E

Q7 A is to B as C it to?

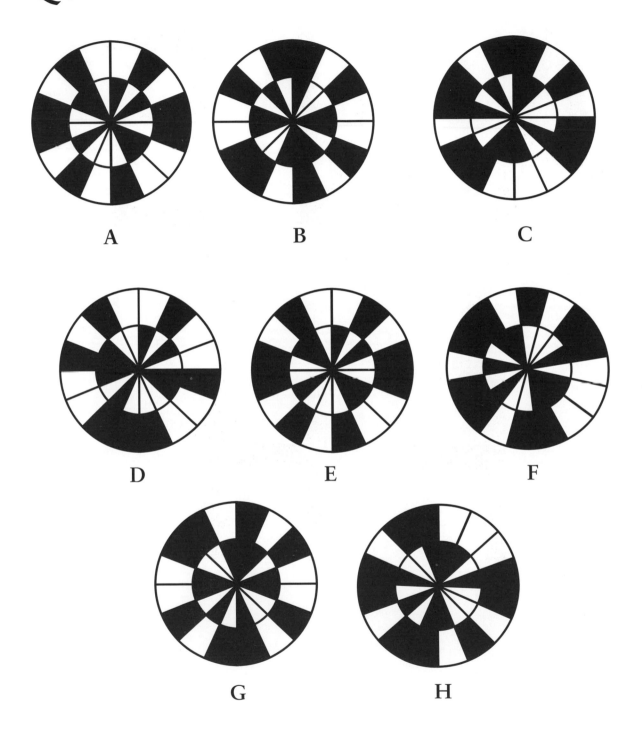

A

B

C

D

E

F

G

H

Q8 Which is the odd one out?

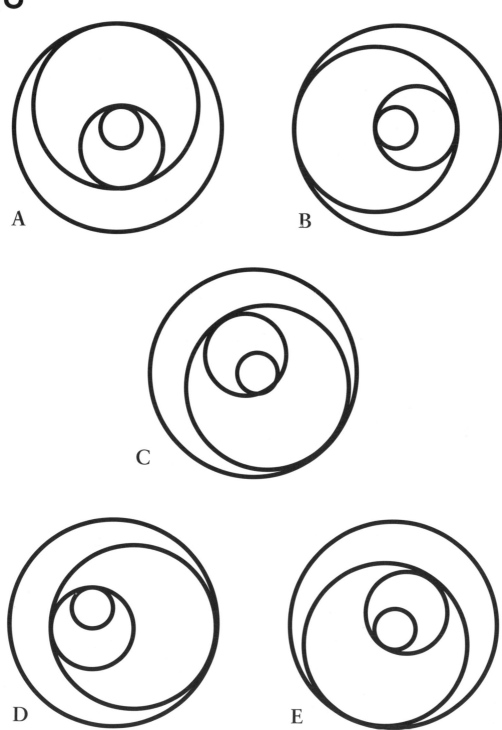

Q9 Which is the odd one out?

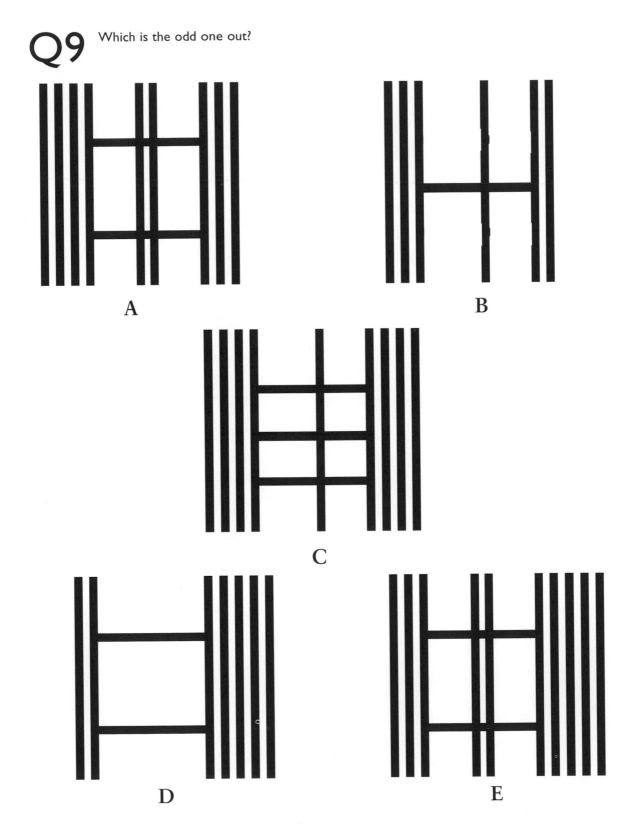

A

B

C

D

E

Q10 A is to B as C is to?

A

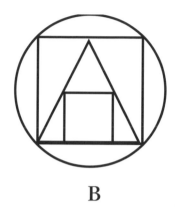

B

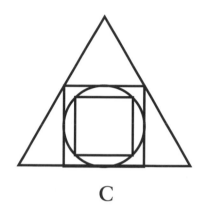

C

D

E

F

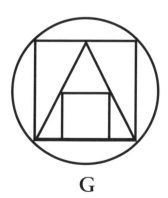

G

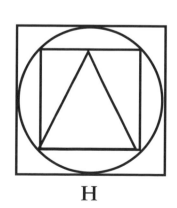

H

Q11 What comes next in this sequence?

L N Q U ?

Q12 ^{A is to B as C is to?}

A is to B as C is to?

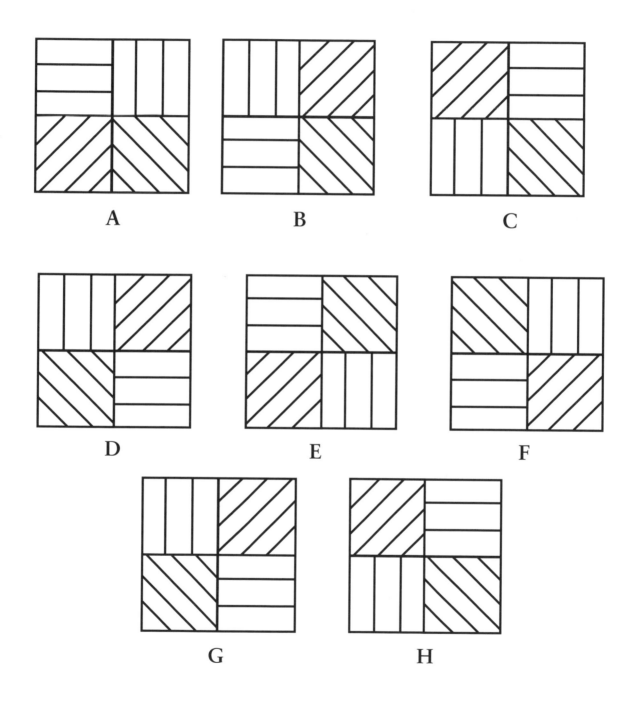

A   B   C

D   E   F

G   H

Q13 Which is the odd one out?

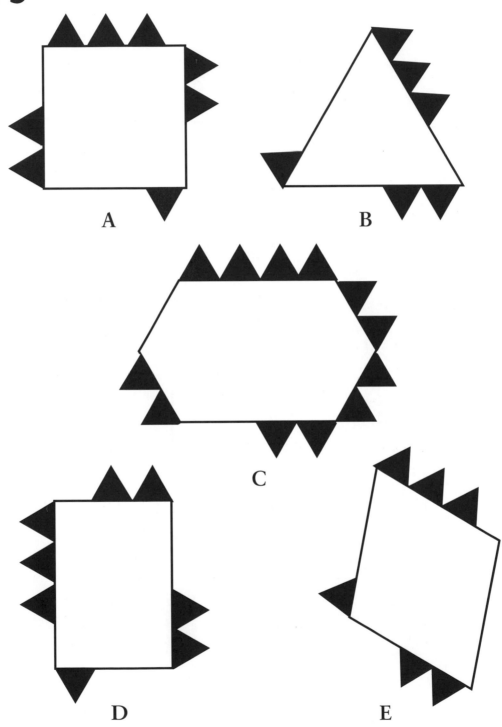

A

B

C

D

E

Q14 Which is the odd one out?

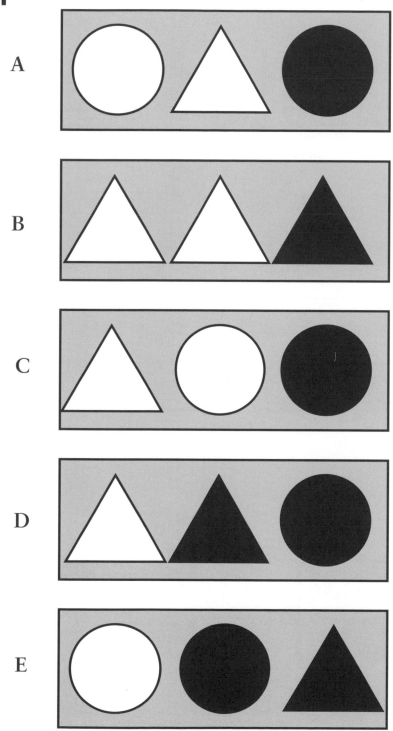

Q15 ^{A is to B as C is to?}

A is to B as C is to?

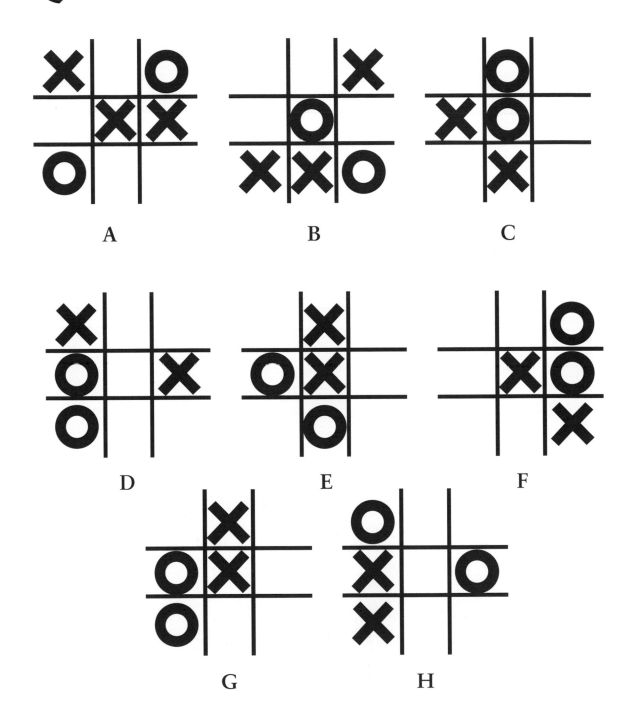

A

B

C

D

E

F

G

H

Q16 Which cube can be formed from this?

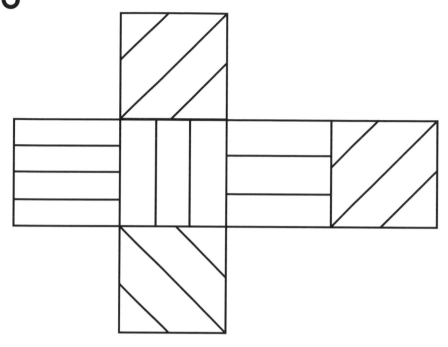

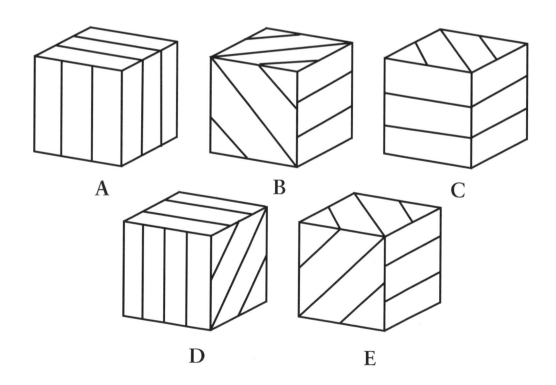

A   B   C

D   E

Q17 Which cube can be formed from this?

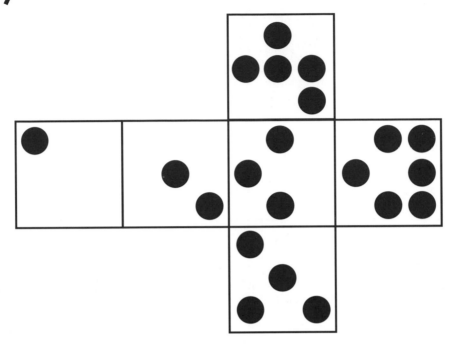

A   B   C

D   E

Q18 Which of shapes fits to complete a square: A, B, C, D or E?

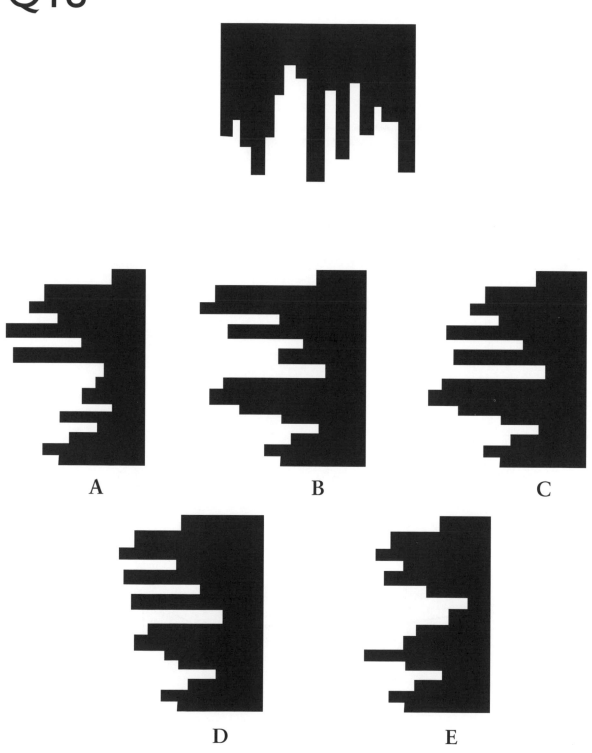

A

B

C

D

E

Q19 What comes next in this sequence: A, B, C, D or E?

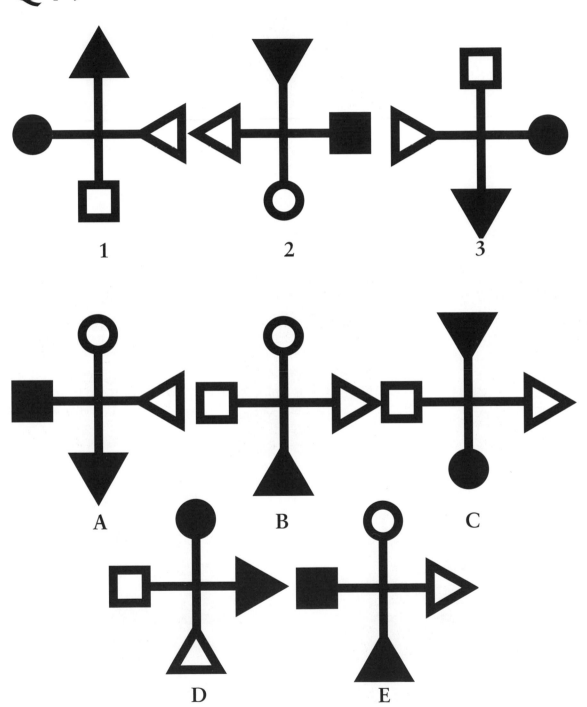

Q20 Which is the odd one out?

A

B

C

D

E

Q21

Which is the odd one out?

A

B

C

D

E

Q22 A is to B as C is to?

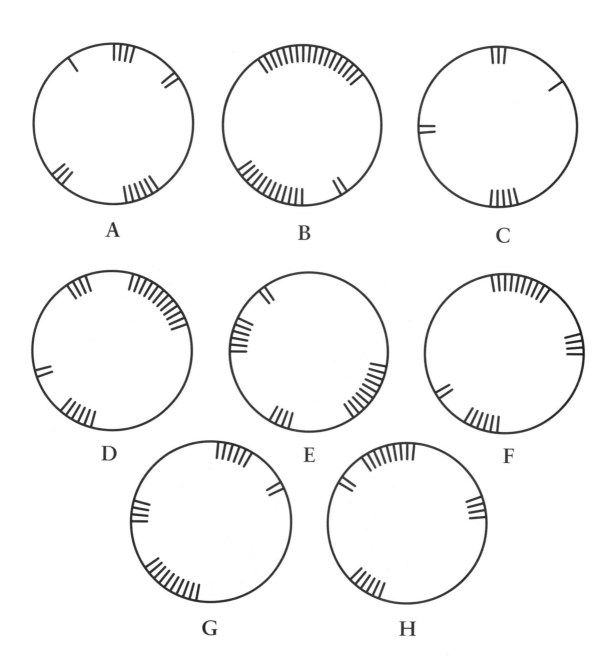

Q23 Which of the following completes the diamond: A, B, C, D or E?

A

B

C

D

E

Q24

Which of the cube layouts folds up to form the cube below?

A

B

C

D

E

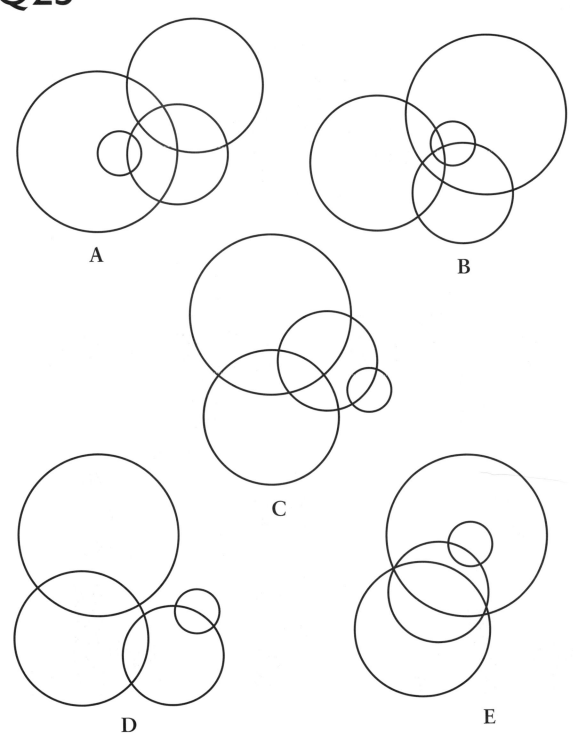

Q25 Which is the odd one out?

A

B

C

D

E

Q26 A is to B as C is to?

A
C
F
T

B
E
I
X

C
D
W
B

D
Z
F
C

E
F
Z
F

F
Y
C
F

G
E
Y
E

H
F
Y
G

Q27 Which is the odd one out?

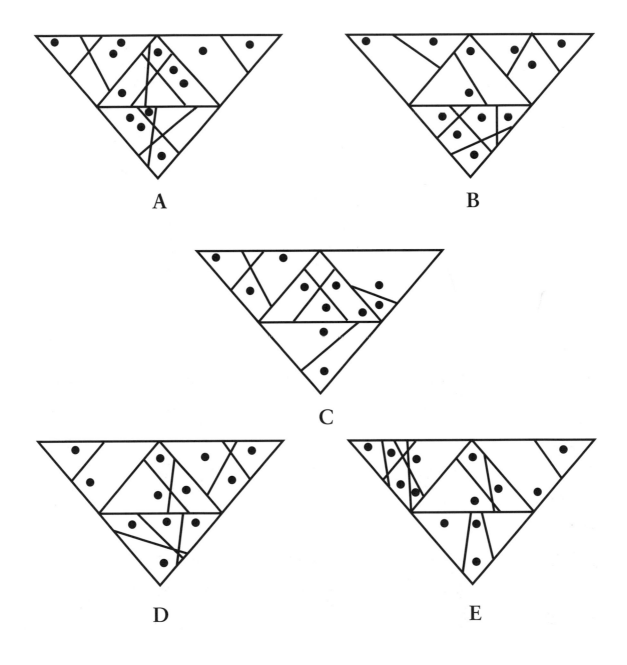

A

B

C

D

E

Q28 Which is the odd one out?

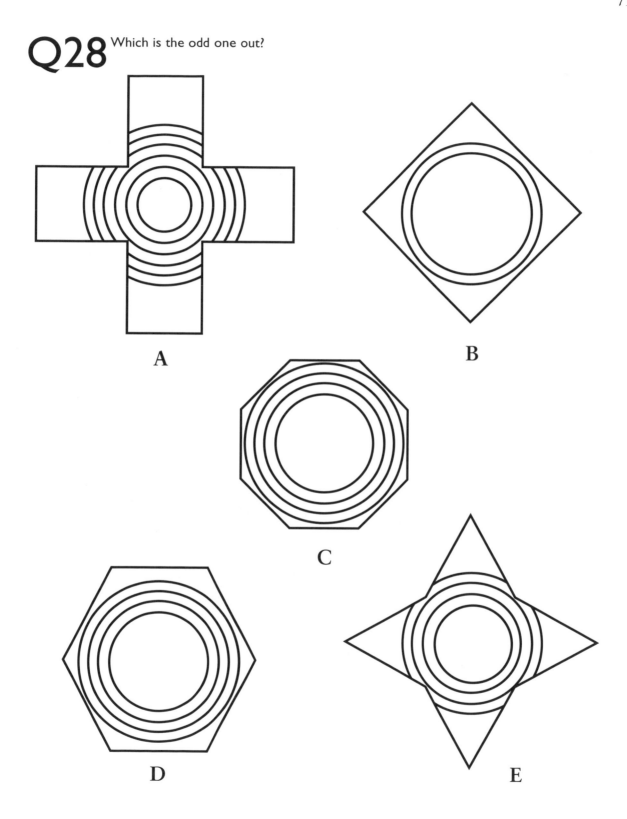

A

B

C

D

E

Q29 A is to B as C is to?

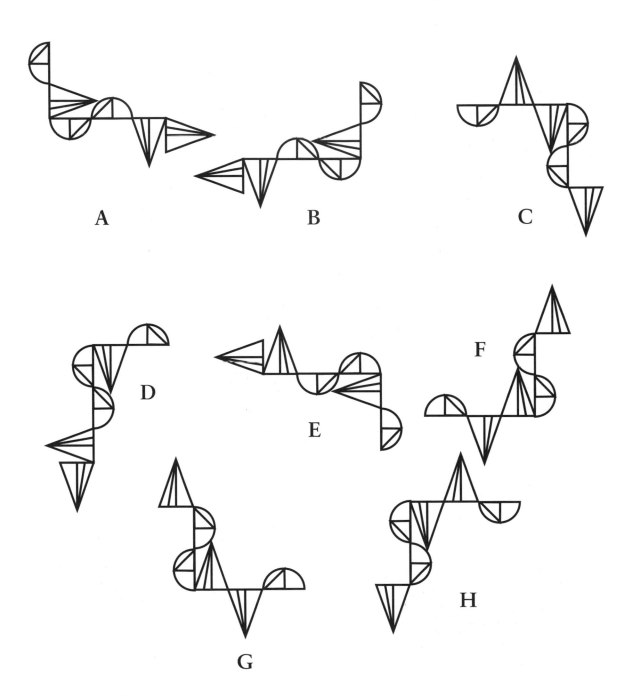

A

B

C

D

E

F

G

H

Q30 <small>Which is the odd one out?</small>

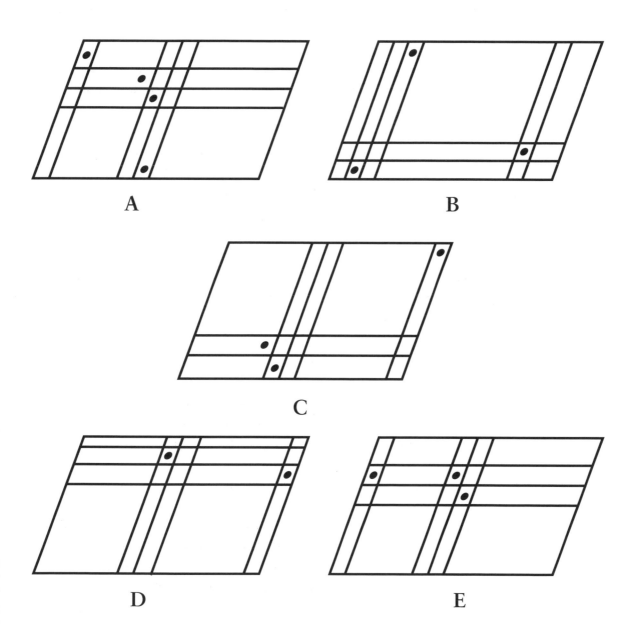

A

B

C

D

E

TEST 1 ANSWERS

A1. B. B lacks the complete triangle formed in the others.

A2. C. Sequence of 90° clockwise rotation; reflection lengthways.

A3. B. 1 black spot changes into 4 white; 2 white spots change into 1 black. String of spots moves round 72° clockwise as sequence progresses.

A4. E. For all the others, the number of white spots multiplied by the number of black spots equals the number of black/white spots on the right.

A5. E. Pattern rotates 90° anti-clockwise. Number of lines alternates between 1 and 2 each time. Shapes alternate between triangle and circle: a triangle is followed by a circle of a different shading colour; a circle is followed by a triangle of the same shading. Arc remains unchanged.

A6. C. All the others are formed from 3 straight lines.

A7. D. White segments change to black; black to white. Pattern is reflected horizantally.

A8. D. For all except D a smaller circle is joined to a larger one on the edge directly opposite the previous join.

A9. E. Vertical lines represent 1 integer; horizontal lines represent 5. The product of the number of lines on each end equals the sum of lines in the middle i.e. 2 horizontal lines intersected by 2 vertical = 10 + 2.

A10. D. Square goes to circle; triangle to square; circle to triangle

A11. Z. Working through the alphabet starting from L, there are 1, 2, 3, then finally 4 letters between each letter.

A12. H. Large square rotates 90° anti clockwise followed by reflection about the horizontal axis.

A13. E. For all except E, the number of triangles surrounding each base shape is a multiple of the base shape's number of edges.

A14. D. For all except D, blank circle = 1; blank triangle = 2; black circle = 3; black triangle = 4. Sum of value of 2 shapes on left equals value of shape on right.

A15. D. Noughts/crosses move 2 spaces working from left to right, top to bottom.

A16. E.

A17. A.

A18. C.

A19. E.

A20. E. Divide each large triangle into four equal medium-sized triangles – the three corners upright, and the center pointing downwards. Apart from in E, each of these medium triangles consists of 2 small black triangles, and 2 small white triangles.

A21. A. For all except A, the total product of the diagonal lines on each corner of each square equals the 'number' in the middle.

A22. F. Circle is rotated 180°; each set of dashes is duplicated adjacent to original set.

A23. E.

A24. B.

A25. E. With the exception of E, circles of

decreasing sizes overlap, with the smaller segment of each circle overlapping on the circle immediately larger.

A26. E. From A to Z, letter in first row moves forward 2 letters; in second moves forward 3; in third moves forward 4.

A27. C. The number of straight lines intersecting each of the 4 smaller triangles within each large triangle is 1 less than the number of dots in the same triangle.

A28. D. With the exception of D, the number of circles is equal to half the number of edges of the appertaining shape.

A29. H. Reflection horizontally.

A30. E. Except for E, only 1 dot appears in each vertical/ horizontal strip.

SCORING

Many people find this sort of reasoning does not come to them easily and, even though they may score highly on other sorts of test, they can struggle with one like this. It is common when invigilating the supervised Mensa test to hear people who sailed through the other sessions groaning with effort over the spatial paper.

OVER 25

If you scored over 25 you are doing superlatively well. This was a tough test and the time limit is exacting. Well done!

20–24

A score of 20-24 is very enviable, though not quite in the genius category.

15–19

Between 15 and 19 you are still showing good reasoning skills but it looks like spatial is not quite your thing.

BELOW 15

Below 15 you have a problem in this area. Don't worry, you are not alone. Spatial skills are not the whole story by a long way, anyway.

TEST 2 NUMERICAL REASONING

There has always been a strong link between the ability to calculate and IQ. Handling numbers effectively is a sure sign of a lively intelligence. However, the reverse is not necessarily true, people who are bad with numbers are not by any means automatically unintelligent. The results of this test should therefore be interpreted with some caution.

TIME LIMIT FOR THIS TEST IS 30 MINUTES

Q1 What comes next in the sequences below?

a) 2, 5, 14, 41

b) 84, 80, 72, 60

c) 58, 26, 16, 14

d) 39, 50, 63, 78

Q2 How long will a box of 72 chocolates last when 6 hungry people each gobble 2 sweets every three minutes?

Q3 Study the square to work out which number should replace the question mark.

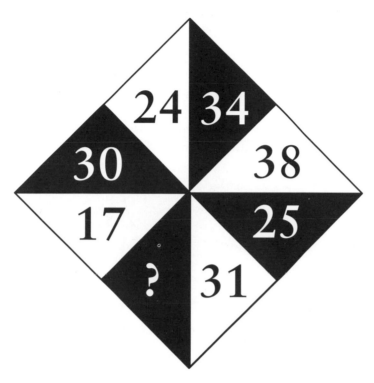

Q4 Which shape replaces the question mark?

Q5 Letters A to D are all assigned to whole numbers. If A is half the value of B, where B equals the square root of C, C being twice the value of D, and the sum of D's two integers equals 5, what are the 2 possible values of A?

Q6 Study the figure below to assign the correct whole numbers or symbols to the letters A - E. You should perform each operation as you encounter it, moving clockwise from the bar to equal 49 in both cases.

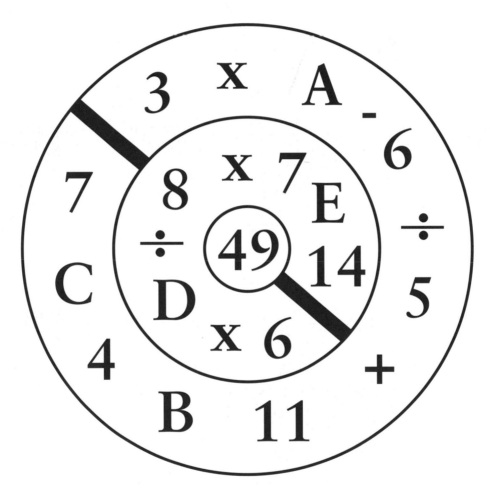

Q7 The Johnsons are guests of honour at a family gathering. They are due to make their grand arrival at 7:30 p.m. Living some distance from the venue, their car journey spans 140 kilometres. They envisage travelling at 90 kilometres an hour for 40 minutes, and an average of 60 for the remaining time. When should they leave to arrive on time, given that they allow an additional 20% of the scheduled journey time for hold ups?

Q8
Using the fact that each of the rows of fours squares sum to the same value, what should replace the question mark?

Q9
If **2R + S - 3T = 9, S x T = 10R** and **2R = S**, what do **R, S** and **T** equal?

Q10

Insert a basic mathematical symbol in-between each number below to make the equations valid. No symbol is used more than once in each equation.

a) $3 \quad 4 \quad 5 \quad 6 = 13$

b) $7 \quad 8 \quad 9 \quad 10 = 125$

c) $11 \quad 12 \quad 13 \quad 14 = 140$

Q11

150 students enrol to study accountancy at the Faye Lynn School of Finance. The examination scoring policy is such that 70% of hopefuls progress to the second year; two thirds of these make it to the third year, and 3 in 14 students fail the final exam. How many of the current intake of aspiring accountants can expect to qualify?

Q12

Study the pyramid of numbers to determine the true values of A, B and C.

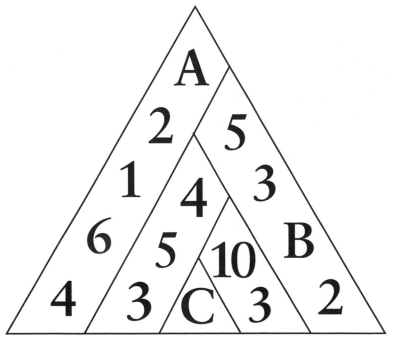

Q13 What one fruit will balance the final set of scales?

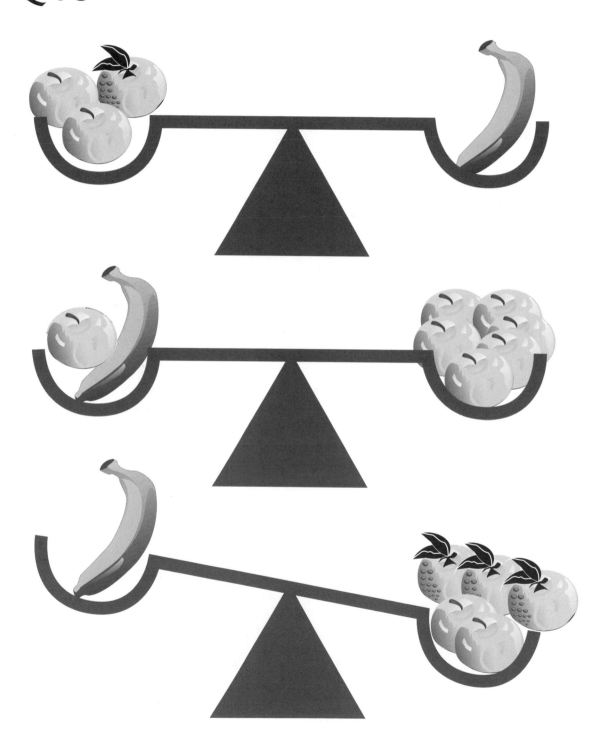

Q14
If ▲ is worth the square root of half of 128, and three ▲s equal the value of ●, what is ■ worth when its value is a quarter of that of ● ?

Q15
What comes next in each of the sequences below?

a) 66, 44, 24, 6

b) 144, 12, 120, 10

c) 22, 29, 43, 64

d) 55, 74, 57, 72, 59

Q16
Lydia banked $1,000 on April 1st 1998 and left it to mature. Fixed annual interest of 8% is earned payable on January 1st each year. Where savings have been invested for less than a year, interest is proportional to the fraction of the year for which the account has been open. How much interest to the nearest dollar has Lydia earned, before tax, when she withdraws her savings on May 1st 2000?

Q17
Examine the relationship between the numbers in the star to discover the value of ?

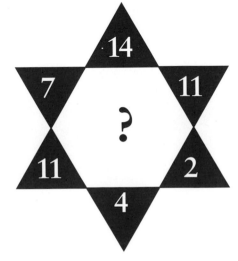

Q18 Sam fills a small tank with a base of 24 x 18cm, and a height of 30 cm two thirds full with water. Being an inquisitive soul, he wants to know the volume of a lead soldier he has just bought. After placing it in the tank, the water level rises to 22 cm high. What is the volume of the soldier in cm³?

Q19 3 friends venture out to hit the summer sales. If Joe's indulgences cost 60% of Mike's, whose shopping amounts to 120% of Liam's, how much have they each spent when the total bill is $730?

Q20 Find the 3 components of the pattern to calculate the number or basic mathematical operation represented by letters A - C.

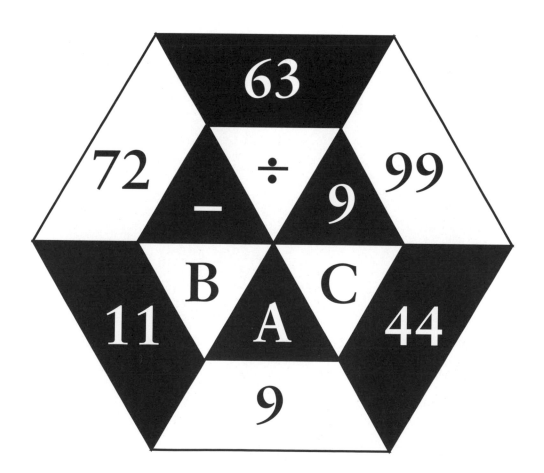

Q21 Luke decides to sharpen up his ten-pin bowling skills. Previous performance has shown that he tends to knock down 4 skittles one quarter of the time on one attempt, 7 two thirds of the time, and 10 otherwise. How many skittles is he likely to have knocked down on average after two attempts?

Q22 An oak tree is planted in a nature preserve. The head gardener wishes to place a protective circular fence around the sapling. The distance from the tree to the fence at any point is 90cm. What area of grass does the fence enclose, when the area of any circle is equal to pi x R^2, where R is the radius, or distance from the circle centre to the edge, of the circle, and pi is approximately 3.14. Give your answer to the nearest cm^2.

Q23 Puzzle over the squares below to determine the true values of A and B.

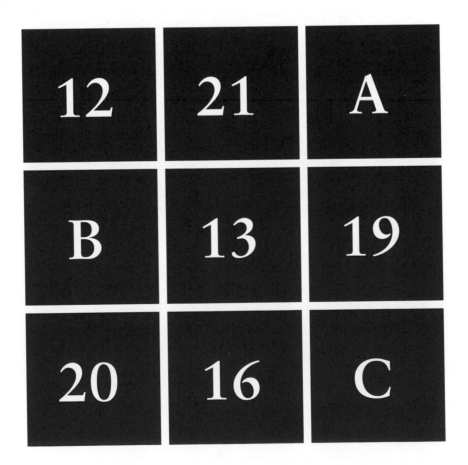

Q24 100g of Minty Marvels cost $2.40 and the pricier Orange Ovals cost twice as much. When 2 Orange Ovals weigh as much as 5 Minty Marvels which themselves weigh in at 10g each, how many Orange Ovals would you get for $3.60?

Q25 Brad is half the age of his father, who is 3 times the age of his niece Imelda. How old is Brad when the three's combined age in years is that of Brad's 88 year old grandmother?

Q26 Pythagorus' theorem states that: $X^2 + Y^2 = Z^2$ where X and Y are the lengths of the two sides of a triangle adjoining a right-angle, and Z is the length of the edge opposite it (the hypotenuse). If X is three quarters of the length of Y, which is 8cm, how long is Z?

Q27 A 366 day leap year occurs once every four years in each year whose year date is exactly divisible by four, except for those century years not divisible by 400. How many times did William Shakespeare (1564 -1616) experience February 29th during his life? (include leap years in the year of birth and death, if relevant)

Q28 Referring to recent questions if necessary, use the dimensions of the triangle to calculate the area of the circle, to the nearest cm².

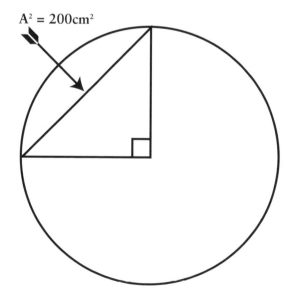

$A^2 = 200cm^2$

Q29
Gizmos and Gadgets Corporation is planning its manufacturing schedule over the coming months. The factory is open for production Monday-Friday each week. Each production run is such that 170 of each product are manufactured. Abcas have a run of 6 days; Bacas one of 5, and Cabas 9. Due to limited resources, only 1 production run occurs at any one time during the 100 days of the schedule. 850 Bacas are produced within this time, and the Abcas run spans 6 working weeks. How many Cabas are produced when all scheduled production time is utilized?

Q30
If the value of each letter of the alphabet corresponds to its position, i.e. A=1, B=2, C=3, ..., what is the square of the sum of the vowels?

TEST 2 ANSWERS

A1. a) 122 (x3 -1), b) 44 (-4, -8, -12, -16), c) 10 (sum each pair of integers, then multiply by 2), d) 95 (+11, +13, +15, +17).

A2. 18 minutes.

A3. 21 sum of pairs of numbers directly opposite to each other equals 55.

A4. Circle - triangle=5, square=8, circle=9.

A5. 4 and 5.

A6. A=7, B=X, C= -, D=12, E= -, where each sum equals 49.

A7. Just after 5 p.m. (5:06 p.m. precisely).

A8.

A9. R=6, S=12, T=5.

A10. a) 3 x 4 - 5 + 6 = 13, b) 7 + 8 x 9 - 10 = 125, c) 11 + 12 - 13 x 14 = 140.

A11. 55.

A12. A=5, B=4, C=15. The product of the numbers in each strip is worth half of the product of the numbers in the immediately longer strip.

A13. 1 banana. Apple=2, orange=4, banana=8).

A14. 6. Triangle=8, circle=24, square=6.

A15. a) -10 (-22, -20, -18, -16),
b) 100 (/12, x10, /12, x10),
c) 92 (add products of 7: +7, +14, +21, +28),
d) 70 (+19, -17, +15, -13, +11).

A16. $145.

A17. 308, the product of the 3 numbers in each of the 2 large triangles.

A18. 864 cm^3.

A19. Joe spends $180, Mike $300, Liam $250.

A20. A=7, B=x, C=28. 3 sums stretching diagonally across the hexagon.

A21. 13.

A22. 25434cm^2 or 2.54m^2.

A23. A=17, B=18, C=14: the sum of the numbers in any horizontal or vertical line equals 50.

A24. 3.

A25. 24.

A26. 10cm.

A27. 14.

A28. 314cm^2.

A29. 850.

A30. 2601. A=1, E=5, I=9, O=15, U=21.

SCORING

OVER 25

Anything over 25 is absolutely excellent and, given good results on the other tests as well, would indicate an extraordinarily high IQ.

20–24

Between 20 and 24 is very good but not on its own indicative of genius. However, the results of the other tests may well make up for any shortcoming on maths. For most people a score in excess of 20 would be a subject for celebration, bearing in mind that, for our present purpose, we are looking for the best of the best.

15–19

A result between 15 and 19 is pretty good for everyday purposes but, in the IQ stakes, not that high.

BELOW 15

Below 15 you are not that proficient with numbers and your numerical reasoning skills need sharpening. The nice thing about this sort of reasoning is that it will improve with practice.

TEST 3 VOCABULARY

A large vocabulary has always been regarded as a sign not only of high intelligence but also of the ability to channel your brain power in useful ways. If you can juggle with verbal concepts, you are likely to be able to handle ideas effectively and communicate them to others with ease. This test is designed to test your word power to the limit. The words are all quite difficult but are all in regular use. We have avoided words that are archaic or only used in dialect. See how many you get right. In each case you must look at the first word in each group and find another word similar in meaning to it.

		A	B	C	D
1.	PRAGMATIC	Political	Accurate	Practical	Civil
2.	EPICURE	Philosopher	Author	Fraudster	Gourmet
3.	GRADATION	Degree	Height	Veracity	Dexterity
4.	HETERODOX	Rigid	Varied	Unfair	Unconventional
5.	SABBATIZE	Ritualize	Confirm	Bless	Organize
6.	ENDEMIC	Popular	Native	Thoughtful	Final
7.	ENDOGAMOUS	Friendly	Matrimonial	Free	Grateful
8.	HASLET	Jerkin	Relation	Entrails	Armour
9.	GALACTIC	Milky	Astronomical	Stellar	Huge
10.	LASSITUDE	Heat	Overeating	Faintness	Verbiage
11.	LEPID	Cool	Weak	Unkind	Pleasant
12.	DARIOLE	Mould	Forge	Decoration	Dagger

		A	B	C	D
13.	FALCATE	Tremble	Crossed	Sickly	Sickle-like
14.	GEMINATE	Doubled	Bejewelled	Flourishing	Growing
15.	MORPHEW	Leaf	Vein	Sacrifice	Skin eruption
16.	PROTOPLASM	Living matter	Organism	Cell wall	Erudition
17.	PROPRIETY	Decency	Rulership	Efficiency	Courage
18.	SESSILE	Fragile	Sedentary	Straight	Pleated
19.	PROSAIC	Thoughtful	Dull	Hopeful	Varied
20.	MONOLITH	Pillar	Arch	Building	Construction
21.	PELTA	Roof	Shield	Sword	Verse
22.	JUGATE	Unusual	Decent	Paired	Forgotten
23.	CRAPULENCE	Dishonesty	Boasting	Sickness	Violence
24.	EXTIRPATE	Destroy	Forget	Flee	Forgive
25.	GESTALT	Recognition	Pattern	Shadow	Area
26.	INCRESCENT	Large	Slow	Bright	Waxing
27.	MORDACIOUS	Biting	Wicked	Extreme	Gleeful
28.	ONUS	Honour	Burden	Rebate	Penalty
29.	COAPT	Dense	Slow	Join	Formal
30.	ESTOP	Cork	Preclude	Terminus	Here
31.	FROTTAGE	Rubbing	Embroidery	Parsimony	Rejoicing

		A	B	C	D
32.	KITH	Relatives	Friends	Knowledge	Peel
33.	GABELLE	Ornament	Jewel	Tax	Toy
34.	DURUM	Wheat	Plenty	Pleasure	Soil
35.	LIMPID	Cold	Poor	Depraved	Clear
36.	MORIBUND	Dying	Poorly	Sash	Belt
37.	PENCHANT	Hanging	Bias	Mirror	Overhang
38.	PUTATIVE	Unconfirmed	Untried	Powerless	Reputed
39.	MEPHITIS	Inflammation	Growth	Stink	Infection
40.	INCHOATE	Angry	Worried	Incomplete	Sideways
41.	GENITIVE	Possessive	Giving birth	Delayed	Productive
42.	JEJUNE	Yellowed	Valuable	Doubtful	Spiritless
43.	FETTLE	Order	Chain	Control	Mend
44.	MORSURE	Bite	Lace	Cinch	Corruption
45.	INVEIGLE	Contradict	Invent	Entice	Dispute
46.	INVEIGH	Humiliate	Forbid	Destroy	Attack
47.	PINION	Wing	Stake	Breath	Consume
48.	NEFANDOUS	False	Gloating	Stolen	Abominable
49.	LENTIGO	Vegetable	Freckle	Mouse	Framework
50.	FABIAN	Indecisive	Cowardly	Delaying	Secret

TEST 3 ANSWERS

1. C	11. D	21. B	31. A	41. A
2. D	12. A	22. C	32. B	42. D
3. A	13. D	23. C	33. C	43. A
4. D	14. A	24. A	34. A	44. A
5. A	15. D	25. B	35. D	45. C
6. B	16. A	26. D	36. A	46. D
7. B	17. A	27. A	37. B	47. A
8. C	18. B	28. B	38. D	48. D
9. D	19. B	29. C	39. C	49. B
10. C	20. A	30. B	40. C	50. C

SCORING

The maximum score is 50.

OVER 45

This is a tough test and if you scored over 45 your vocabulary is absolutely excellent. You probably work with words professionally and solve crossword puzzles with an ease that infuriates your friends.

35–44

If you scored between 35 and 44 your score is still very good indeed. You have a vocabulary well outside the normal range.

25–34

A score of 25-34 is extremely creditable and would indicate quite a good command of the language.

15–24

A score of 15-24 would be about average. The test did contain quite a few common words which, though you might not use them every day, would be in the vocabulary of an educated person.

BELOW 15

Below 15 you need to work on your word power.

TEST 4
VERBAL REASONING

FLEX YOUR VERBAL DEXTERITY WITH THE TEST BELOW. TIME LIMIT IS 5 MINUTES.

1. Brick is to House as Branch is to:
a) Wood　　b) Tree　　c) Hut　　d) Mouse　　e) Flower

2. Wet is to Arid as Sick is to:
a) Healthy　　b) Right　　c) Malady　　d) Sane　　e) Dry

3. Apple is to Tomato as Turnip is to:
a) Carrot　　b) Bread　　c) Plum　　d) Avocado　　e) Bowl

4. Pestle is to Mortar as Motte is to:
a) Water　　b) Building　　c) Peat　　d) Forest　　e) Bailey

5. Vapour is to Precipitation as Cocoon is to:
a) Cold　　b) Exterior　　c) Pupa　　d) Spray　　e) Silk

6. Bambino is to Adult as Sapling is to:
a) Oak　　b) Branch　　c) Wood　　d) Tree　　e) Table

7. Culmination is to Start as Summit is to:
a) Peak　　b) Base　　c) Height　　d) Snow　　e) Mountain

8. Stale is to Originality as Compromise is to:
a) Concede　　b) Lie　　c) Resolute　　d) Agree　　e) Apologize

9. Marathon is to Stamina as Fire is to:
a) Smoke　　b) Flame　　c) Light　　d) Fuel　　e) Ash

10. Leaf is to Book as Yolk is to:
a) Bond　　b) White　　c) Egg　　d) Hen　　e) Hatch

11. Effeminate is to Man as Tomboy is to:

a) Bairn   b) Girl   c) Gentle   d) Balance   e) Straight

12. Depilate is to Hair as Mow is to:

a) Cut   b) Field   c) Soil   d) Grass   e) Trim

13. Temperature is to Degree as Distance is to:

a) Metre   b) Remote   c) Time   d) Space   e) Separate

14. Material is to Tangible as Theory is to:

a) Rule   b) Abstract   c) Argument   d) Explain   e) Idea

15. Challenge is to Stretch as Elongate is to:

a) Shrink   b) Question   c) Dismiss   d) Lengthen   e) Multiply

Are you well warmed up now? Stretch out with another word work out: spot the imposter in each of the groups below.

16.   a) Conformist   b) Orthodox   c) Traditionalist   d) Dissident   e) Acquiescent

17.   a) Supercilious   b) Contemptuous   c) Denigrating   d) Laudation   e) Depreciating

18.   a) Tradition   b) Reformation   c) Revolution   d) Innovation   e) Transposition

19.   a) Incessant   b) Unremitting   c) Resistance   d) Sustained   e) Continual

20.   a) Proficient   b) Punctual   c) Competent   b) Capable   e) Ambidextrous

21.   a) Captive   b) Detainee   c) Trusty   d) Prisoner   e) Custodian

22.   a) Coerce   b) Compel   c) Coalesce   d) Enforce   e) Bludgeon

23.   a) Duce   b) Autocrat   c) Despot   d) Tyrant   e) Riposte

24.   a) Retaliate   b) Avenge   c) Enforce   d) Requite   e) Recompense

25. a) Enumerate   b) Paginate   c) Calculate   d) Cipher   e) Figure

26. a) Idiosyncrasy   b) Eccentricity   c) Foible   d) Mannerism   e) Philanthropy

27. a) Classify   b) Categorize   c) Rank   d) Compile   e) Place

28. a) Median   b) Mainstream   c) Midrib   d) Equidistant   e) Centre

29. a) Patter   b) Lingo   c) Index   d) Dialect   e) Idiom

30. a) Premeditated   b) Spontaneous   c) Makeshift   d) Improvised   e) Impromptu

TEST 4 ANSWERS

1. b	**2.** a	**3.** a	**4.** e	**5.** e	**6.** d	**7.** b	**8.** c	**9.** d
10. c	**11.** b	**12.** d	**13.** a	**14.** b	**15.** d	**16.** d	**17.** d	**18.** a
19. c	**20.** b	**21.** e	**22.** c	**23.** e	**24.** c	**25.** b	**26.** e	**27.** d
28. b	**29.** c	**30.** a						

SCORING

OVER 25
25 or over is excellent.

OVER 20
Over 20 is very creditable.

15–19
This would suggest that your verbal skills need attention.

BELOW 15
Below 15 suggests problems in this area.

CREATIVITY

Creativity and originality of thought are traits intrinsic to genius. But as we have already discussed, these skills may be of little consequence in isolation. Topicality and plausibility are both prerequisites for any blast of creativity to be attributed to genius, along with a sheer determination to persist regardless of any setbacks.

Creativity can be interpreted in different ways. Eminent talents already mentioned boast different skills: Shakespeare (literary), Einstein (scientific), Mozart (musical). The questions below aim to gauge your creative abilities, but you should recognize that your creativity may also be manifested in different forms. Judge for yourself by having a bash at the following tests, but remember: one bright idea does not necessarily elicit genius.

Do you have a creative personality?

These questions are intended as a quick taster - judge for yourself the creative subject matter closest to your own heart.

1. Do you find brainstorming:

a) tortuous – you find it difficult coming up with ideas quickly.

b) stimulating – you find your mind working quicker than your pen can.

c) useful, especially with others – you are most able to bounce ideas around when others contribute their own and help take yours forward.

2. During the course of daily grind, be it following a recipe or attempting a bit of DIY, does the lack of a listed material result in you:

a) feeling frustrated and searching for a substitute. Attempts to adapt procedures by using the substitute usually go wrong.

b) going out to buy the exact material required before continuing.

c) effortlessly adapting to either making the most of what you have or quickly reaching for a substitute. You generally reach the desired result.

3. You purchase something requiring simple home assembly, but later discover the instructions are in Japanese (and you're a little rusty). Are you most likely to:

a) lay out all the components and figure out what goes where and how. It usually works.

b) contact the retailer and demand comprehensive English written instructions. Otherwise, ask for a refund.

c) elicit some help from a willing, practically-minded friend.

4. Do you find works of art:

a) boring. You can't understand the point of them, and find it difficult to gauge their quality.

b) fascinating. You find it easy to lose yourself in the imagery of an abstract painting and able to offer various interpretations.

c) interesting but your attention span is limited. You tend to buy the guidebook to facilitate understanding of different works.

5. Popular belief states that everyone has a novel hiding in them somewhere. Does the prospect of writing a book leave you:

a) excited. You love words and enjoy expressing yourself with a colourful vocabulary. You find it easy to imagine storylines and fantasies.

b) challenged. Much as you would like your fifteen minutes of fame, you would seek much of your inspiration from past experience. Filling a whole book would take some considerable time and effort.

c) uninspired. You may enjoy reading, but would prefer to leave the effort of writing to some other more imaginative soul.

6. Which of the following typical types of examination question do you prefer:

a) a specific question with multiple choice answers.

b) an open-ended question open to different interpretation and answerable in an essay format.

c) questions relating to, and applying information/ facts given in the question.

7. Which of the following activities do you find the most fulfilling:

a) watching television.

b) reading.

c) writing.

8. For the musicians amongst you, when playing your chosen instrument, do you prefer to:

a) read sheet music and adhere to the manuscript.

b) improvise with a group of like-minded musicians.

c) play by ear, reproducing what you've heard, embellishing wherever possible.

9. Struck by an idea provoking you to ask why hasn't someone thought of/ done that before, are you most likely to:

a) action your idea with a bit of research and deeper thought, initiating some lively debate if nothing more tangible is possible.

b) shrug it off, deeming it not worthy of further thought, preferring to think about lunch instead.

c) engross yourself for a while longer in your thoughts before getting distracted – your intention to return to it is normally in vain.

10. Do you consider yourself:

a) innovative – you dislike following rules and tried and tested methods and procedures.

b) a follower – you prefer to follow the accepted method of doing something, but are willing to lend your support to others' ideas if convinced of their validity.

c) indifferent – you are a laid-back, relaxed individual who just 'goes along with whatever'.

CREATIVITY SCORING

The higher the score, the higher the creativity

1.	a) 0	b) 2	c) 1
2.	a) 1	b) 0	c) 2
3.	a) 2	b) 0	c) 1
4.	a) 0	b) 2	c) 1
5.	a) 2	b) 1	c) 0
6.	a) 0	b) 2	c) 1
7.	a) 0	b) 1	c) 2
8.	a) 0	b) 2	c) 1
9.	a) 2	b) 0	c) 1
10.	a) 2	b) 1	c) 0

SCORING

Maximum Score is 20

17-20
This would suggest that you are a highly creative person with plenty of original ideas.

13-16
This is a very good score which could be improved with practice.

9-12
This suggests that you need to work hard on improving your creativity.

BELOW 9
This indicates that creativity is really not your strong point.

CREATIVE BRAINSTORMING

These tests have no right or wrong answers. The knack is to go right on thinking until you get to some really new and creative ideas. Don't be satisfied with the first ones that you think of as these will undoubtedly be the same as everyone else's. Where you will really score will be when you persist up to the point where you think you can find no more ideas – and then, quite unexpectedly, you will.

Cast your mind over the list of objects below and break away from convention: dedicate three minutes to scribbling down as many possible uses for each as possible. Let your imagination flourish – physical limitations are not an issue!

1. A wooden spoon
2. A baseball cap
3. An inflatable tyre
4. A wire clothes hanger
5. A 20m rope
6. A chimney
7. The Statue of Liberty
8. A table football game
9. The resurrected *Titanic*
10. The White House

On a more visual note, take a look at the series of abstract images to the right and jot down as many interpretations of each as possible. There are no right or wrong answers – this is an exercise to explore how laterally and creatively you analyze what confronts you. The more you come up with, the better!

PRACTICAL PUZZLERS

Use your powers of creativity to attempt the following challenges – this time there is a more practical dimension to them. The whole point of creativity is the originality of thought and performance. There is not always a neat solution – there may not be one at all, there may be just one, there may be many. Hence it's up to you to decide how you fare: are you satisfied with your performance? Are you lost for ideas or do you perhaps find that you lack the time to implement them all?

Equip yourself with some sheets of paper and a pair of scissors. Can you make a box which holds itself together without adhesive?

Keep hold of the scissors and get a postcard/ postcard sized piece of paper. Can you cut it in such a way that you are able to climb through it so your entire body passes through? It should remain in one piece...

Place 12 matches in front of you. Use as many of them as you like at one time to emulate a recognizable form e.g. a fish outline. How many can you create in 10 minutes?

Raid the kitchen to discover how many "musical instruments" you can make from the utensils on offer. Even better if you can create your own mini symphony!

For the more literarily inclined, arm yourself with a pen and paper and as much time as you desire. Then start on your novella. But not before studying the list below: your storyline must smoothly incorporate as many of these objects/events as possible, in whatever order. You have up to 500 words to complete your narrative. Enlist a friend or relative to act as critic if you deem yourself somewhat partial: the main criterion is how imaginatively you have written your work, but the storyline must flow well and be as enthralling as possible for the reader. Here your ability to be creative is tested alongside that of your dedication to follow an idea through and implement it successfully. The more events you include the better – but points deducted for incongruities!

1.	A cat	8.	Tuesday
2.	A candle	9.	Euro currency
3.	A gas explosion	10.	Chocolate cake
4.	The sea	11.	A motorbike
5.	Family relationships	12.	Solar panels
6.	A saucepan	13.	A telephone bill
7.	A cello	14.	An examination
		15.	Rain

CONCENTRATION

'If you want to be Pope, you must think of nothing else.'
Spanish proverb

To be effective, genius needs concentration. You can't be an effortless genius, it just doesn't work. There seems to be a strong correlation between concentration and creativity. This is something that happens in the subconscious and is not well understood, but people who do creative work of any sort will recognize it immediately. If you concentrate hard upon your project and work at it with all your effort you will find that, once you stop, your subconscious continues to wrestle with the problems and will often present you with solutions at the most unusual times. It also comes up with completely unexpected solutions. This is the really odd bit. You discover that your subconscious can think up things that your conscious mind would not have discovered. The effect can be exciting but not a little spooky. But it only works if you have concentrated hard beforehand. Sitting waiting for inspiration is like sitting waiting for lightning to strike.

Thomas Edison showed an admirable example of concentration before he managed to find a suitable material for the filament of his electric lightbulb. He tested literally dozens, maybe even hundreds of substances to see which was the most suitable. Because what he was doing was new, he had no idea what sort of material would be able to glow with enough intensity without burning out.

> **Typically it was Edison who said that genius is 1% inspiration and 99% perspiration. That was certainly true of his type of genius.**

We've seen how important concentration is, but how do you get it? Do you remember at school how the teachers used to yell, 'Concentrate!', but never told you how? It's one of those things people expect you to know, yet most of us are very bad at it. However, when you find someone with real concentration, it is impressive. My German friend Sonny can read a book with so much concentration that she is oblivious to the outside world until she's finished. She can knit a sweater at one sitting without thinking about anything else. Wow! I wish I could do that.

Look at the number of works composed by Mozart, or the subjects explored by Da Vinci, who was famous for his exploration of engineering, anatomy and architecture alongside his skills as an artist. In order to deliver this level of output, their lives must have been highly focused, with resolute powers of concentration. As you have doubtlessly discovered when engrossed in something yourself, concentration levels are largely proportional to how interesting you find the subject matter. The odds on discovering Mozart had an aversion to music are untenable! So the better your ability to concentrate, the more you will absorb and widen your knowledge and the higher the chance that you reach your full potential/invent a miracle cure/write a masterpiece. So, what affects your capacity for concentration and how can you improve it?

Environmental considerations

The environment in which you work can have a devastating effect on your ability to focus. Ask yourself:

Are you too hot or too cold?

If you're busy shivering, it is unlikely your attention is focused fully on the task at hand. Too hot, and you may be feel more inclined to doze off.

Are you being disrupted by noise?

If children are running around shouting, music is playing loudly, the telephone rings constantly, you are less likely to maintain a sharp focus. Of course, you may find some level of background noise conducive to concentration, but too much can be detrimental. Consider moving rooms, reaching a compromise with the noisy offenders,

turning the music down, shutting your windows – or even wearing ear plugs. If none of these options are available, then at least try and accept the noise and address your feelings of frustration. It may reflect the fact that you have convinced yourself you cannot work in the prevailing surroundings, rather than being the physical disturbances themselves.

Is there sufficient light?

Insufficient light can provoke tired and sore eyes, be soporific, and elicit undue effort. A lamp over your work area can not only provide better light, but also help physically focus your attention. Good daylight and light bulbs which simulate daylight are more conducive to concentration than other electric lights and are less likely to instigate feelings of staleness and lethargy.

Is there adequate ventilation?

A stuffy and poorly ventilated work area may cause breathing difficulties, tiredness and discomfort. The more physically you are at ease, the greater will be your powers of concentration.

Is your work area free of clutter?

You are less likely to maintain clarity of thought and vision if surrounded by clutter and rubbish. If you are in the process of working on different projects, try to keep the work physically separated. This will encourage you to focus on the current task and minimize the chance of being distracted. Maintaining order in your work environment can contribute to a similar level of clarity in your head.

Does your work area exist exclusively for that purpose?

In addition to the clutter of the previous point, be aware that any association your work area has with another activity is likely to distract you from its current purpose. Trying to study whilst lounging on your bed might well instigate a greater desire to fall asleep; working in the kitchen could inspire you more to explore the contents of the refrigerator rather than the solution to the world's problems. Keeping an area set aside exclusively for your work can act as another physical focus, even if it just means using a particular chair.

Is your table/instrument/easel at the correct height or position?

Minimize any physical discomfort. You'll know it's right when you don't even think about it.

Are you wearing comfortable, non-restrictive clothes?

Too comfortable and relaxed and you may find your mind feels likewise. Experiment – if you find it difficult to concentrate whilst trying to work at home, donning a suit may lessen the urge to be distracted and go and clean the bath!

Subject matters

The more engrossed you are in a subject, the less likely you will need to address your level of concentration. But given that most people tend to have a plethora of thoughts and concerns to hand at any one time, here are some suggestions to help a straying mind stay focussed:

"But it's boring!"

The subject matter may be less than scintillating, but as with everything, it's what you make it. If you're undertaking a dull task, think: can you do it more efficiently? Ask yourself the reason why you're doing it: view it as the means to an end if necessary, the perspiration before the inspiration. Can you inject some humour into the task to make it more interesting? Have you categorized it as boring before even giving it a chance?

"I mustn't forget to feed the goldfish…"

Total concentration is unlikely if your mind is overrun with the monotonies of everyday life, or other projects. Before embarking on a major task, take a few minutes to jot down a "to do" list so you can shut out these distractions, and not be burdened with the "I mustn't forget" syndrome.

Plan ahead

A new project or vision may seem highly daunting, especially if of a complex nature. It may instigate a tendency to not know "where to start", and feelings of confusion and resignation, both likely to hinder any attempt to concentrate – thus the emphasis on a plan. Of course, if you're stretching creativity to its limits, you may not know where your work will lead you. But if a more structured approach can be taken then consider the stages you will take and how you will attack each one. Then as you tackle each in turn, you will be focused on that precise issue and less prone to being distracted with the "bigger picture".

Speed reading

If, like many others, you find your attention wandering when reading and have no recollection of the last paragraph, then you may find it useful to address your reading skills. The quicker you read, the less likely you will lose focus, but too quick and you may skip words and fail to fully digest the text. Practice reading newspaper articles and making a note afterwards of the main facts without referring to the text. This will help you absorb what is important and disregard the more trivial. A useful technique is that of viewing text as a series of groups of words rather than a mass of single words. Try reading three or four words at a time in one glance, and then the next block, and so on. Though demanding of some effort initially, you will be able to build up the number of words in each group and read quicker as a consequence. In addition, training your eye to absorb the key words will facilitate a deeper understanding and recollection of what you have read.

Take a break

Listen to your body. Tiredness may be at the root of an inability to concentrate. Taking a break can alleviate fatigue and introduce a fresher outlook. Exercise can be a great help – a brisk walk can invigorate and provide an active thinking ground; a swim can aid concentration in itself with its subconscious attempts to regulate breathing and movement.

What whiff?

The profuse presence of aromatherapy is there to be sniffed at: Japanese companies have examined the effect of circulating certain smells around the offices via air conditioning systems. Both lemon and mint have been found to stimulate concentration and productivity. Try it for yourself.

First try this test to see how well you think you concentrate.

Find yourself a quiet corner and try and banish everyday concerns from your mind. Now get started. Consider the following situations, and select (honestly!) the response you would most likely adapt.

I. During the course of everyday conversation, how often do you find yourself asking "now, where was I?":
a) Never.
b) Often.
c) Occasionally.

2. You're ploughing through a challenging scientific article. Are you most likely to:
a) Drift off into a daydream early on and give up to avoid wasting more time.
b) Focus wholeheartedly on the text and absorb fully most of what you've read.
c) Manage a few minutes before realizing you don't know what you've just read and have to recap.

3. Imagine yourself working in a busy, open plan office. Would you find yourself:

a) Able to shut out the many distractions, forcing yourself to focus entirely on the task at hand.

b) Highly unproductive – your attention would wander to the noise and movement around you.

c) Able to work in short bursts, with attention lapses here and there.

4. Do you work best:

a) With a steady hum of background noise.

b) In any environment – you rarely notice what is or isn't going on if you're deep in thought.

c) In total silence.

5. You're watching a rather dull documentary relevant to your work. How much are you most likely to absorb and remember afterwards?

a) Little – you "switched off" early on in proceedings.

b) The majority – you would have a good overall picture with a handful of hard facts to quote.

c) A more fragmented impression – your mind has a tendency to wander.

6. Would you describe yourself as:

a) Having a good attention span – if you need to focus, you will.

b) Able to apply yourself and your attention to stimulating subject matter, but less so for the more mundane.

c) Unable to concentrate wholeheartedly on anything for more than a few minutes at most.

7. After being introduced to a fellow guest at a party, are you most likely to:

a) Find yourself surreptitiously asking for a reminder a little later as you failed to take his/her name in the first time.

b) Remember the guest's name a week later without prompting.

c) Get the name half right a bit later – your mind was not entirely focused on the pleasantries.

8. You have been commissioned to write a lengthy article on a topic close to your heart. With a week to complete the work, would you:

a) Start immediately, able to maintain clarity and work efficiently to finish well before the deadline.

b) Procrastinate for a few days and then rush the article off, working through the night to meet the deadline.

c) Set yourself a rigid timetable, adhered to most of the time, but sometimes you find yourself unable to focus and in need of a break.

9. Does everyday life find you most likely to be:

a) Dashing constantly between jobs, leaving some unfinished as you flit from one thing to another.

b) Focusing entirely on the job at hand and finishing as much as possible before embarking on something else.

c) Focusing on more than one thing at a time – it may take a little longer than doing each individually but at least you don't get bored.

10. Do you find yourself daydreaming:

a) Regularly – and not without some considerable embarrassment.

b) Rarely – you are usually too focused on whatever you are doing at the time.

c) Sometimes – but only when you find yourself doing something particularly tedious.

11. How often have you been asked a question and been compelled to ask for it to be repeated as you weren't listening?

a) A few times.

b) Frequently.

c) Rarely, if ever.

12. Would you find taking the minutes of an interminable meeting:

a) Rather onerous, but your mind would be on the job.

b) A task requiring considerable effort to minimize the inevitable inaccuracies you make.

c) Impossible – you would never be able to concentrate on everything and are much more proficient delegating the job to someone else.

13. How often do you find yourself muttering "it's no good, I just can't concentrate"?

a) Regularly – regardless of the environment you are in.

b) Sometimes – normally provoked by some intrusive physical disturbance.

c) Rarely – you are adept at applying yourself whenever you deem it necessary.

14. You're working on a challenging and rather convoluted project in a team. Are you most likely to be the person:

a) Trying in vain to focus your fellow team members on the task, loath to digress.

b) Trying to "liven things up" – whether dropping in a tasty morsel of gossip or suggesting a coffee break.

c) Contributing to the discussion now and again, having to refocus whenever you realize your mind has wandered.

15. How often do you find yourself slamming on the brakes of your car or stopping yourself in your tracks when you realize your concentration has lapsed and someone is in your way?

a) All the time.

b) Now and again.

c) Hardly ever.

16. You receive some surprising (but not troublesome) news of a personal nature. Next day at work are you:

a) Able to carry on as normal, blocking out the revelations until your working day is over.

b) Of little use – your mind is buzzing with the news and attempts to concentrate on work are futile.

c) Slightly less productive than normal – attention may wander, but once you realize this, you revert your focus to work.

17. Do you find deadlines:

a) The cause of much anguish – despite attempting to focus on the task, you find yourself distracted by continually determining how much time you have left.

b) Of little consequence – depending on your level of interest, you generally find it easy to settle down and work until a task is completed.

c) A helpful motivator – the nearer the deadline, the better you can concentrate as you realize the work has to get done.

18. You find yourself embroiled in a verbal conflict: your partner swears s/he told you something of which you have no recollection and claim s/he didn't. Is it most likely that:

a) You were told but you weren't paying attention at the time.

b) Your partner is confused and actually told someone else – you always listen attentively.

c) You were told but immediately deemed it of no consequence and have since forgotten.

19. You are undertaking an arduous calculation with the help of your calculator where you must sum a long string of numbers. Is this:

a) Slightly frustrating – you find yourself having to do it again as you forgot where you were.

b) A nightmare – you find yourself unsure as to whether you have entered certain numbers and end up doing it six times before getting two totals which tally.

c) Unproblematic – you ensure you are uninterrupted and feel confident with your first result.

20. You spend a relaxing evening watching a gripping thriller with a web of sub-plots running through. Are you likely to:

a) Have a decent overall idea of the storyline, but remain a bit unsure of the complete picture.

b) Be bombarded with questions demanding to know what's going on as you're the one most likely to know.

c) Be the one doing most of the bombarding.

SCORING

	a	b	c		a	b	c		a	b	c
1.	2	0	1	8.	2	0	1	15.	0	1	2
2.	0	2	1	9.	0	2	1	16.	2	0	1
3.	2	0	1	10.	0	2	1	17.	0	2	1
4.	1	2	0	11.	1	0	2	18.	0	2	1
5.	0	2	1	12.	2	1	0	19.	1	0	2
6.	2	1	0	13.	0	1	2	20.	1	2	0
7.	0	2	1	14.	2	0	1				

SCORING

The maximum score is 40.

35–40

You obviously have excellent concentration and are able to bring your full mental faculties to bear on any task that confronts you. This ability to focus your effort so sharply will undoubtedly be of the greatest assistance in your quest for genius.

28–34

You concentrate well but you could do with improvement. Try the exercises in this section to see if you can increase your level of ability.

20–27

You concentrate quite well but are distracted too often. You are allowing your mental effort to be frittered away on silly things which don't matter. Work hard at the exercises and you will see a really worthwhile improvement.

UNDER 20

Your concentration is really quite... Erm, would you PAY ATTENTION when I'm speaking to you?

Getting better

Most of us don't consciously practice concentrating. Try to think about what you are doing. Decide when you start a task that you will concentrate on it until you have finished. Choose to work in a place where you will not be distracted. Make sure you are comfortable (warm enough in winter, cool enough in summer, plenty of fresh air, etc). Rather than work for a while, then make yourself a coffee, then get up to see if the mail has arrived, and then return to the work when you have lost the thread of what you were doing, try planning your work. Split your task into blocks of work and decide to concentrate on each block until it is finished. Reward yourself with a coffee or whatever when you have finished a block.

As I writer I work in units of 1,000 words. If things are going well then, by the time I've finished my first thousand, I'm ready for a coffee. The second thousand earns me lunch. When I've reached my quota for the day I feel I've earned a couple of glasses of wine in the evening.

You may find this way of working hard to begin with, especially if you're not used to it, or you have colleagues who keep dropping in for a chat. Be firm with yourself and everyone else. If people want to chat make sure they do it over the coffee that you awarded yourself for work done.

The phone is a curse when it comes to concentrating. It rings at the most inconvenient times and then people expect you to talk about things that completely destroy your train of thought. If you can, put the answering machine or voice mail on for an hour or more at a time. Then set aside time to listen to your messages and return important calls. This way you will avoid being interrupted repeatedly and having your whole work session turned into a fiasco.

Try this

This is a technique for building up concentration that is still taught by Buddhist monks in the Far East. It has been used for hundreds, maybe thousands of years and is still very effective. Take a lighted candle and set it on the table in front of you. Sit comfortably looking at the candle and relax as much as possible. Concentrate on all the details of the candle – colour, shape, size, the way the flame moves – make sure you notice every tiny thing about it. Now close your eyes and try to visualize the candle. You'll find to begin with that you can only hold on to the mental image of the candle for a very short time. After a few seconds you may have an *idea* about how a lighted candle looks but you will have lost the picture of that particular candle. Open

your eyes and try again. You will find that with practice you can hold the image of the candle for longer and longer periods of time. The ability to do this will start to affect your concentration generally. You will find that you can rivet your attention on one task so completely that you are oblivious to distracting influences.

There is a saying among Hassidic scholars that you should be able to concentrate on your work so hard that a beautiful 18-year-old (of your preferred gender) could stand naked beside your desk and you wouldn't notice. OK, so no one said it was going to be easy. As for me, I've just finished this section and earned myself a coffee...

PRACTICAL TEST 1

O K, now you believe that you know your level of concentration. You have also practiced some exercises to help you improve that level. So here is the test that will show you what you have achieved. Take all the time you want. This test is about extreme accuracy, not speed.

The grid of numbers may look meaningless, but your task is to scan each line and count the number of consecutive pairs of numbers which sum to 10. Count 1 each time you unearth such a pair and mark 1 dash on a piece of paper each time you have counted 10 pairs of numbers in your head. In addition, mark a different dash every time you find yourself having to re-scan a line. At the end, count the number of pairs you have found using your dashes, and your score is the difference between the exact number of pairs and your count (assign a positive number regardless of whether you have too many or too few). Then add the number of times you have re-scanned and you have your score for the test. To find out how you did, divide your score for this test by 10 and subtract that amount from 40, then cross-check it with the results table on page 108. The number of pairs you should have found is at the foot of page 112 overleaf – and no peeking!

COUNTING MARKS

```
5 1 3 6 9 8 7 6 4 5 4 5 4 6 4 5 4 6 6 4 5 7 8 3 7 3 7 2 8 3 9 1 9 5 6 7 6 8 5 1
5 5 6 5 4 5 4 5 5 8 2 8 2 8 3 9 5 6 4 7 9 5 7 6 2 4 7 4 8 5 2 1 5 4 9 7 3 6 2 6
5 7 8 9 1 4 3 6 9 6 7 3 5 7 9 7 9 4 6 6 7 6 4 3 8 7 9 8 2 3 1 6 8 1 8 7 3 6 9 7
8 1 3 5 7 9 7 9 7 3 8 3 8 2 8 2 2 3 9 4 9 4 9 2 9 8 2 3 8 4 2 5 6 9 7 5 6 7 6 7 5
5 5 4 5 4 5 6 4 6 4 5 8 5 9 2 4 7 5 9 6 9 2 1 4 8 7 8 4 6 9 5 7 9 2 1 7 4 3 9 1
1 5 7 8 9 8 9 8 2 5 3 4 6 9 5 8 2 3 7 3 7 8 9 7 8 9 2 8 7 9 5 6 9 1 9 8 5 8 4 2
8 4 9 5 6 7 2 3 8 5 8 5 9 2 1 7 8 9 3 1 6 5 6 5 5 5 8 6 9 8 7 5 8 9 8 1 8 5 8 5
4 8 4 9 4 6 4 6 8 9 5 3 9 4 3 2 5 7 9 8 9 5 9 2 9 1 3 4 6 4 9 5 8 5 8 4 9 2 3 7
1 5 7 9 8 2 9 1 9 8 5 9 5 8 9 4 3 6 5 9 1 9 5 3 5 4 6 9 8 9 2 8 5 5 4 5 4 6 9 8
1 9 1 8 2 8 1 9 8 1 2 8 9 1 9 8 5 8 2 4 9 7 8 2 8 3 9 4 5 9 8 1 2 5 4 2 9 8 5 9
1 9 5 8 5 9 2 9 3 4 9 8 7 3 4 5 4 6 5 4 5 4 9 8 2 9 5 4 9 8 5 3 2 4 9 8 5 9 7 2
5 5 4 5 8 5 9 2 9 1 9 5 2 6 4 7 9 3 4 5 8 9 2 5 4 9 5 3 7 9 5 6 4 8 2 9 5 9 1 4
6 5 8 9 4 9 5 2 9 3 6 4 9 5 8 5 9 8 9 4 5 6 6 4 9 8 5 9 8 5 3 5 6 4 9 8 2 1 6 5
8 4 9 5 8 6 9 4 3 6 5 4 9 8 5 8 9 2 3 1 3 1 3 2 1 2 5 2 5 2 4 2 6 8 2 9 5 8 9 5
8 4 9 7 5 8 5 8 5 4 9 8 5 9 2 9 6 4 5 4 9 8 2 9 2 3 1 6 5 8 5 8 2 9 6 4 9 8 2 8
5 4 9 8 7 9 5 8 2 8 2 5 9 4 9 2 9 8 5 9 1 5 1 9 1 9 5 8 6 4 9 4 8 7 2 7 2 9 8 4
5 1 6 1 8 4 9 2 4 9 5 8 7 6 4 1 9 5 9 3 4 6 4 9 8 2 8 5 9 4 2 6 5 7 2 7 5 9 9 1
3 4 1 9 7 5 5 4 9 5 9 8 4 6 4 6 6 5 9 4 8 2 9 8 2 9 1 9 5 9 5 9 5 5 8 5 9 9 4 9
1 3 1 5 1 9 4 8 7 5 7 6 7 9 8 2 9 8 6 4 6 1 3 1 5 1 6 4 9 1 9 5 8 7 3 4 6 1 9 5
8 2 4 9 4 8 6 5 7 3 1 9 1 9 8 4 3 7 3 7 5 9 4 8 2 8 6 4 5 9 1 9 1 9 5 9 1 9 5 8
3 1 6 1 9 8 2 4 9 5 4 6 7 5 8 7 3 2 9 5 8 4 9 7 3 5 8 8 4 9 4 8 4 9 1 5 8 7 3 9
2 1 3 1 8 5 4 9 7 6 7 5 9 8 2 8 4 9 5 7 6 2 8 2 9 4 9 3 5 4 6 4 9 1 9 1 9 7 3 7
2 4 6 5 9 8 7 3 7 5 7 9 7 8 4 8 5 9 5 5 4 6 4 5 4 6 4 5 6 4 9 8 2 9 8 2 9 4 9 8
1 9 8 4 3 7 2 7 5 8 8 5 4 6 2 9 8 7 3 7 5 9 8 4 6 8 5 2 9 5 6 9 1 9 8 4 9 7 3 9
5 5 5 4 9 4 8 4 6 4 9 8 1 8 2 5 4 6 4 9 8 1 8 4 3 7 3 9 4 6 5 9 3 1 6 1 5 1 9 4
1 6 5 4 9 7 2 8 5 8 4 9 5 6 7 3 2 8 5 9 4 9 8 5 6 7 8 9 5 9 1 9 1 9 5 9 8 7 9 4
6 4 6 5 8 7 9 1 9 5 8 2 8 3 4 6 5 9 1 8 4 9 7 8 5 8 4 9 5 9 1 3 2 6 4 9 4 6 5 6
3 2 6 4 9 8 2 7 2 7 3 5 9 5 9 1 9 5 6 4 6 9 9 6 9 3 9 6 4 6 5 9 4 8 7 6 1 4 6 5
3 6 4 6 5 9 7 5 8 2 8 5 6 4 9 4 9 5 3 6 4 9 8 7 6 5 9 1 9 5 8 6 4 9 5 9 4 6 4 9
1 6 1 6 5 9 4 9 4 8 2 8 5 8 6 4 9 5 9 7 3 2 9 5 9 9 4 4 9 8 8 9 7 9 5 8 5 8 5
5 5 4 5 5 4 5 5 6 6 5 6 4 6 5 8 2 8 5 8 9 5 9 1 6 4 6 5 9 7 6 5 9 4 9 5 9 1 1 9
3 2 6 2 6 9 8 3 8 3 6 5 9 2 9 8 5 9 7 8 5 8 5 8 2 8 2 8 5 8 5 6 4 9 5 9 7 3 8 8
3 2 6 2 6 5 9 8 7 9 8 5 8 6 8 6 8 9 5 9 8 2 3 4 6 6 5 6 5 5 6 6 5 6 5 9 8 8 9 5
1 3 1 6 5 8 8 2 5 8 9 4 9 5 6 6 4 7 7 3 7 3 5 6 1 5 1 1 6 5 6 1 6 5 6 1 1 3 5 6
6 5 6 4 9 8 3 7 9 8 9 5 9 5 9 8 6 4 9 5 8 2 9 1 9 1 9 5 6 5 9 4 9 8 6 7 6 5 9 2
3 1 3 2 5 8 7 3 7 3 6 9 6 5 9 5 9 1 9 5 8 2 6 3 6 4 6 5 9 8 3 8 3 6 9 5 9 4 3 1
1 3 5 3 5 3 6 4 6 9 8 5 8 9 5 9 5 9 4 9 2 9 5 8 6 7 6 3 6 9 3 4 3 4 8 3 4 8 4 3
3 1 3 7 3 7 5 8 2 8 2 9 5 9 1 9 4 6 5 5 8 5 8 5 5 5 5 2 3 4 6 4 9 8 7 3 7 6
3 1 3 1 2 1 8 1 6 4 9 4 9 8 2 8 2 8 2 2 5 6 4 9 8 5 6 7 9 5 9 8 1 6 4 6 5 4 6 2
```

PRACTICAL TEST 2

Now on to a test of verbal concentration. The following excerpt from Charles Dickens' classic *A Tale of Two Cities* is littered with deliberate type errors. Put your powers of concentration to the test by reading through and counting how many you find. You may read each line only once, but you have no time limit, so work at the pace that you find most comfortable. Bear in mind that the slower you read, the longer the task will take, and so the higher the chance that your concentration will wander. Again, you can take all the time you want, but be ACCURATE.

"A suspennded interest and a prevalant absense of mind were perhaps obserrved by the spies who looked in as the wine-shop,, as they looked in at every place, high and low, from the kings palace to the criminal's gaol. Games ab cards languished, players at domiinoes musingly built towers witht hem, drinkers drew figures on teh tables with spilit drops of wine, Madame Defarge herself picked out the pattern on her sleeve with his toothpic, and saw an heard something inaudaible and invisible a long way of.. Thus, Saint Antoine in this vinous feature of his, until miday. It was high noontide, when too dusty men passed through his streets and under his swinging lamps: of whom, one was Monsieur Defarge: the other a mender of roads ina blue cap. all adust and athirst, the two enterered the wine-shop. There arrival had lighted a kind of fire in the brest of Saint Antoine, fast spreading as they came along, which stirrred and flickered in flames ob faces at most doors and windows. Yet, no one had followed them, and no man spoke when they entered the wine-shop, thought the eyes of every man there where turned upon them.

"*Good-day, gentlemen!* said Monsieur Defarge.

It may have been a signall for loosenning the general tongue,. It elicited an answering chorus of "*Good-day!*"

"*It is bad weather, gentlemen,*" said Defage, shaking his head.

Upon which, every man looked at his neighbour, and then all cast down their eyes and sat silentt. Except one man, who; got up and went out.

"*My wife,*" said Defarge alowd, addressing Madame Defarge; "*I have travelled certain leagues with this good mender of road, called Jacques. I met him – by accident – a day and a half's journey out of Paris. She is a good child, this mender of roads called Jacques. Give him to drink, my wife!*"

A second man got up and went out. Madame Defarge set wine before the mender of roads called Jackes, who doffed his blue cap to the company, and drank. In the breast of his blouse he carried some course dark bread;, he ate of this between whiles, and sat munching and drinking near Madme Defarge's counter, A third man got up and went out.

Defarge refreshed himself with a draught of wine – but, he took less than was given to the stranger, as being himself – a man to whom it was no raritie – and stood waiting until the countryman had Made his brekkfast. He looked at no one present, and no one now looked up at him; not even Madame, Defarge, who had taken up her knitting, and was at work.

"*Have you finished your repast, friend?*" he askied, in due season.

"*Yes, thank you.*"

"*Come, then! You shalll see the apartment that I told you you you could occupuy. It will suit you two a marvel.*" "

There were 60 errors. Did you find them all? Your score for this test is equal to the number of errors you missed. As in the previous test, subtract your score from 40 and turn to page 108 to find out what your results mean.

Answer to Practical Test 1 – There are 308 pairs.

THINGS TO DO

There is really no way to become a genius. Either you're born that way or you're not. To be honest, if you're reading this book, then probably you've missed the bus as far as genius is concerned. You should be too busy with your world-shattering ideas to bother about books like this.

However, do not despair, for there *are* things you can do to make the very best of the abilities you have. This chapter is designed to show just how to squeeze the last ounce out of the talent you have.

DIET

What you eat has a profound effect on your mental ability and there are a number of things you can do that will increase performance. The first things are quite obvious. You should eat a healthy balanced diet that includes plenty of fibre, fresh fruit and vegetables. Did Shakespeare eat burgers? Exactly! Seriously, although people know these things because they've been told them again and again, many still ignore the advice. You know that if you don't maintain your car it will break down. Your body is a million times more complicated than your car and can do far more amazing things, so why don't you look after it? If you 'fed' your car on the wrong fuel it would ruin the engine. Try it. Go on, see just what happens! No, of course you won't, you aren't stupid after all. But I bet you'd eat junk food

and expect to get away with it, wouldn't you? OK, genius, out with the burgers, fries, donuts and pizzas! In with the fruit, vegtables and cereals.

There are some specific things to do when you're working. Don't, for example, try to work on a full stomach. You'll be mentally and physically lazy after a meal. Rest after eating and only get back to work when you've had time to digest. Don't drink alcohol when you need to work, you may think it relaxes you but in fact it's a depressant and it slows down and confuses your mental processes. Also alcohol destroys blood sugar which not only gives you a bad case of the munchies, but also makes you feel less happy. What you really need when you're working hard is a higher blood sugar level. You can achieve this with the judicious use of sweets. Better still, take a glucose tablet (the sort athletes use before an event): this is very easily absorbed and therefore gives you a rush of energy which can be used for either physical or mental effort.

Stimulants such as tea or coffee can help (they don't call them stimulants for nothing). However, caffeine is a drug and it has side-effects to which some people are more susceptible than others. If you find that caffeine makes you feel jumpy, increases your heart rate significantly (or even gives you palpitations), or deprives you of sleep, then don't use it.

DRUGS

There is a long love affair between some members of the artistic professions and drugs. Even in the 19th century, writers experimented with opium because they knew it could give them access to a world of ideas that they could not enter otherwise. This is not just a bit of silly self-indulgence. The problem with artistic work is that the very best ideas don't come on command. You can't sit down and decide to think up that immortal tune or pen those words of wisdom just when you want to. There is an area of the mind which produces such work but it is the most awkward, cussed and unpredictable part of the mental process. In order to get some kind of contact with this area of the mind, people have resorted to a variety of methods but drugs have been one of the favourites.

The history of what is coyly called 'substance abuse' in recent years is so familiar that it hardly needs to be re-told here. What is important from our point of view is that many highly creative people have believed that the use of drugs could help them unleash creative powers they were unable to reach by other means. The problem is drugs are both illegal and dangerous. For every musician you can point to who drew inspiration from drug-induced states you can think of a hundred more who were held back by drug abuse.

Is there another way of getting inspiration without taking risks with your health or a nasty encounter with the law? Yes, fortunately there is. We have all experienced that place just on the edge of sleep where amazing visions come to us unbidden. These are every bit as vivid as the visions experienced by drug users but they come free, are entirely legal and won't wreck your health. The trouble is that they tend to be intermittent and unpredictable. So what can we do about that?

The first remedy is quite a simple one. You keep a notebook and pen by your bed. When you wake up at night you must immediately write down any thoughts or dreams you can remember, whether or not they make any sense at the time. This is most important. Things that you recollect from the twilight area between sleep and wakefulness are messages from your subconscious and are very important, even if you don't understand them straight away. So write down every detail in a notebook and, from time to time, go through it and see if anything you have written rings a bell. Also keep the notebook with you during the day and write down any stray thoughts or flashes of insight that seem useful. It is surprising how these nuggets of inspiration crop up unexpectedly at times when you're busy with something else. Unless you are ready to catch them they tend to get forgotten.

You can also try a technique that Salvador Dali, the surrealist painter, favoured. He would settle down to take a nap in a comfortable armchair. However, on the floor beside him he would place a metal bowl and just above it he would hold a spoon in his hand. As he drifted off to sleep he would drop the spoon and the clatter as it hit the bowl would wake him up. He found this a very effective way of gaining access to that area of being half-asleep and half awake in which the best and most imaginative ideas are often found.

ARTISTIC KNOWLEDGE

1. Which famous school of Art and Design was founded at Weimar in 1919 by architect Walter Gropius?

2. Which rival of Reynolds earned fame and favour for his society portraits whilst coveting a passion for landscape?

3. By which name is Charles-Edouard Jeanneret better known?

4. Which French painter was highly esteemed not only for his great romantic works but also his extensive journals?

5. Which art movement was led by Picasso and Braque in the early 20th century?

6. What is the name of a three-dimensional sketch in clay or wax prior to undertaking a larger and more precise sculptural work?

7. Which Austrian Expressionist painter was influenced by Klimt, acclaimed for his portrait painting, and died young in the influenza epidemic of 1918?

8. By what name is the 1960s abstract art movement concerned with creating and exploring visual illusions known?

9. Which leading Impressionist is renowned for his studies of ballet and horses?

10. What style of architecture was prevalent in Britain during the 18th century, named after a 16th century Italian architect?

11. Which 19th century English landscape painter worked exclusively in watercolour before turning to oils, using his extensive travels to inspire his liberating, abstract and vibrant work?

12. What name lends itself both to a standard 36 x 28 in canvas and a portrait showing the head and one hand?

13. Which ill-fated painter studied art in Paris and used the art of lithography for his work depicting scenes from theatres, music halls and cafes?

14. Which technique pattern dyes fabrics using a wax resist process?

15. What French term was attributed to a group of young painters whose notoriously bold and vivid work was first shown together in Paris, 1905?

16. Which prolific 20th century Spanish artist showed exceptional talent and expression from an early age, epitomized by Guernica (1937), a work expressing his abhorrence and revulsion of war?

116

17. What name describes the type of architecture utilizing local material and attuned to local needs, generally traditional in its style and of unknown authorship?

18. What Danish architect won international acclaim for his design of the Sydney Opera House?

19. Which liberating movement with a penchant for the bizarre, subconscious and irrational, was founded by André Breton in 1924?

20. By what collective name, indicative of their exploration of the effects of blobs of paint, were the rebellious group of 19th century Italian painters better known?

21. Which term refers to the art of the East Roman Empire from 5th century A.D. to 1453 and the fall of Constantinople?

22. Which Czech painter and designer achieved fame for his distinctive Art Nouveau designs, particularly those of the actress Sarah Bernhardt?

23. Which French painter worked alongside Pisarro and devoted himself to landscape painting, with fame and reverence arriving late on in his life?

24. What name is given to the technique employing gradations of contrasting light and shade in order to model shape and form?

25. By what name is the Italian artist, trained by Verocchio, whose pioneering talents embraced science, anatomy, engineering and architecture, known?

26. What style of furniture and decoration is associated with George IV and early 19th century Britain?

27. Which Spanish architect and designer displayed great originality in his unconventional and fantastical work, epitomized by the church of Sagrada Familia in Barcelona?

28. What artistic trend inspired European artists and writers to explore the gritty reality of everyday life in the 19th century?

29. The notoriety of which exponent of American Pop Art stems predominantly from Campbell's soup and Brillo soap-pad boxes?

30. What term was deprecatingly awarded to 17th and 18th European art and architecture which now describes the style prevalent between that of Mannerist and Rococo?

LITERARY QUIZ

A knowldege of literature may not be proof of genius but, on the other hand, you would expect a genius to have a pretty good knowledge of his or her competitors. This test is tough but, if you have pretensions to literary greatness, you'll need to do well in it. If you're the scientific type we'll let you off. For now.

1. Which poet, known as the Golden Boy, killed himself and, in doing so, gave rise to a famous painting?

2. Who wrote of, "Merely innocent flirtation, not quite adultery but adulteration"?

3. Who wrote, "Mordre wol out; that se we day by day"?

4. Which Shakespeare king said, "I wasted time and now doth time waste me."?

5. Who wrote a huge work in several parts entitled, *In Search of Lost Time*?

6. Which imaginary castle was created by Mervyn Peake?

7. Which book features a desert island, some lost choir boys, and a pig's head on a stake?

8. Which English novel of the Revolution takes place in Paris and London?

9. Who wrote of a slough called Despond?

10. Which brothers were immortalized in a novel by Dostoevsky?

11. Which English novelist wrote: "England's not a bad country... It's just a mean, cold, ugly, divided, tired, clapped-out, post-imperial, post-industrial, slag-heap covered in polystyrene hamburger cartons."?

12. Who compiled the first English dictionary?

13. Which author was primarily responsible for popularizing the legend of King Arthur?

14. Who wrote *The Magic Mountain*?

15. In which book did Maugham write, "People ask you for criticism, but they only want praise."?

16. From which epic poem (and by whom) do these lines come: "The infernal serpent; he it was, whose guile stirred up with envy and revenge, deceived the mother of mankind."

17. Who wrote *The Dunciad*?

118

18. Tennyson wrote a poem named after a royal personage. Who was it?

19. Who wrote,"Rose is a rose is a rose, is a rose."?

20. Who says in which play by which author, "To lose one parent, Mr Worthing, may be regarded as a misfortune, to lose both looks like carelessness."

21. Who wrote an ode entitled *Intimations of Mortality*?

22. By what name did Samuel Langhorne Clemens find literary fame?

23. Which Philip Roth novel featured a notorious piece of liver?

24. According to Mark Twain familiarity breeds contempt – and what else?

25. In which book is it said, "All animals are equal but some animals are more equal than others."?

26. In which novel of the future would you find Bernard Marx and a Native American ?

27. Who wrote *Prometheus Unbound*?

28. Who wrote,"There is no greater pain than to remember a happy time when one is in misery."?

29. Which novel begins, "Last night I dreamt I went to Manderley again."

30. Which woman author wrote a series of novels about Ancient Greece?

ANSWERS

1. Chatterton. 2. Byron (in Don Juan). 3. Chaucer. 4. Richard II. 5. Proust. 6. Gormenghast. 7. Lord of the Flies. 8. Dickens' 'A Tale of Two Cities'. 9. John Bunyan in 'The Pilgrim's Progress'. 10. The Brothers Karamazov. 11. Margaret Drabble. 12. Dr Samuel Johnson. 13. Sir Thomas Malory. 14. Thomas Mann. 15. 'Of Human Bondage'. 16. John Milton, 'Paradise Lost'. 17. Alexander Pope. 18. 'The Princess'. 19. Gertrude Stein (in 'Sacred Emily'). 20. Lady Bracknell in Oscar Wilde's The Importance of Being Earnest'. 21. Wordsworth. 22. Mark Twain. 23. 'Portnoy's Complaint'. 24. Children. 25. 'Animal Farm' by George Orwell. 26. 'Brave New World'. 27. P.B. Shelley. 28. Dante. 29. 'Rebecca' by Daphne Du Maurier. 30. Mary Renault.

SCORING
ART / LITERATURE

25-30
Excellent. You can at least sound like a genius!

20-24
You have a wide knowledge of art/literature.

15-19
Not bad, but not great.

10-14
Average.

BELOW 10
You're not a literary or artistic culture-vulture.

MUSIC QUIZ

You may not know much about music but, in the search to be a well-rounded individual, you should have at least a passing knowledge of some of the greatest works ever produced by the human mind. Try this quiz to see how you shape up.

1. Who wrote the opera *The Rape of Lucretia*?

2. Under which name is Bruckner's Fourth Symphony known?

3. Which of Bach's compositions is an exploration of counterpoint?

4. Which of Franck's symphonic poems is about a count eternally chased by demon because of going hunting on the Sabbath?

5. Who wrote the *Glagolitic Mass*?

6. In which film did the Adagietto from Mahler's Fifth Symphony feature?

7. From which Puccini opera does the tune *Nessun Dorma* originate?

8. What is Tchaikovsky's Seventh Symphony known as?

9. What male character sings a bird-like part in *The Magic Flute*?

10. Which of Haydn's symphonies is known as the *Farewell Symphony*?

11. Who wrote *Fantasia para un gentilhombre*?

12. In which Verdi opera does the character Manrico appear?

13. Who wrote the libretto to *Don Giovanni*?

14. What is the name of the heroine in Tchaikovsky's *Eugene Onegin*?

15. What is unusual about Beehoven's Eighth's Symphony?

16. Under which name is Mozart's Symphony K.385 known?

17. How many symphonies did Sibelius write?

18. Which part of Smetana's *Ma Vlast* desribes the river flowing through Prague?

19. Who wrote the opera *Ariadne auf Naxos*?

20. Which of Verdi's operas focused on an Ethiopian slave girl?

21. What is the name of the prison governor in Beethoven's *Fidelio*?

22. What is the name of Stravinsky's ballet that started his neo-classical period?

23. Under which name is Schuman's First Symphony known?

24. Who wrote the song cycle *Die Schone Mallerin*?

25. Which Wagner opera contains the character Hans Sachs?

26. Which orchestral suite contains *Anitra's Dance*?

27. Who wrote the symphonic poem *The Noonday Witch*?

28. Which composer produced the most successful orchestration of Mussorgsky's *Pictures at an Exhibition*?

29. From which opera does the *Dance of the Polovtsian Maidens* originate?

30. What is the final part in Wagner's *Der Ring des Nibelungen*?

ANSWERS

1. Benjamin Britten. 2. The Romantic. 3. The Art of Fugue. 4. Le Chasseur Maudit. 5. Leos Janacek. 6. Death in Venice. 7. Turandot. 8. Manfred. 9. Papageno. 10. No 45. 11. Joaquin Rodrigo. 12. Il Trovatore. 13. Lorenzo da Ponte. 14. Tatyana. 15. It contains no slow movements. 16. Haffner. 17. Seven. 18. Vltava. 19. Richard Strauss. 20. Aida. 21. Pizarro. 22. Pulcinella. 23. Spring. 24. Franz Schubert. 25. The Meistersinger von Nurnberg. 26. Grieg's Peer Gynt Suite No. 1. 27. Antonin Dvorak. 28. Maurice Ravel. 29. 'Prince Igor' by Alexander Borodin. 30. Gotterdammerung.

SCORING

The maximum score is 30.

25–30

Excellent. At least you have a good knowledge of the works of genius, even though you might not yet have produced any yourself.

20–24

Still very good. The quiz isn't easy and you have acquitted yourself with honour.

15–19

Music is not your preferred area but, even so, your general knowledge is quite reasonable.

10–14

A bit of study might help here. Your knowledge is really quite sketchy and could do with improvement.

BELOW 10

Music is not for you. Try something else.

PHILOSOPHY

Philosophy has always been close to the heart of genius. It deals with the secrets of existence, the *why* of life. If you have any pretensions to genius you should feel comfortable with the great works of the philosophers.

1. Which Greek philosopher supervised the education of the young Alexander of Macedon (later to be Alexander the Great)?

2. Which Breton philosopher, author of *Know Thyself*, is mainly remembered for his tragic love affair and subsequent castration?

3. What name is given to the Theory of Knowledge?

4. What name is given to the study of the nature of being?

5. Who stated, "Cogito, ergo sum"?

6. Which branch of philosophy deals with the nature of morality?

7. Who wrote *The Critique of Pure Reason*?

8. Which pupil of Socrates wrote *The Republic*?

9. What name is given to the moral view that the only thing that is good is pleasure?

10. With which philosophy would you associate Kierkegaard, Sartre, and Heidegger?

11. Which philosophical term originally meant 'the art of conversation, discussion or debate'?

12. Which American linguist wrote *Language and Mind* in 1968?

13. With which philosophy do we associate Diogenes?

14. What name is often given to the employment of methods based on practical experience rather than on an accepted body of theory?

15. Which Scot wrote *A Treatise of Human Nature* in 1737?

16. Who is regarded as the foremost philosophical and religious figure of Ancient China?

17. Which German philosopher lived in the late 17th and early 18th centuries, invented a calculating machine which won him membership of the Royal Society in Britain?

122

18. Which Somerset-born philosopher wrote an *Essay Concerning Human Understanding*?

19. Which philosopher was born in Amsterdam of Jewish parents and was brought up to speak Spanish, Portuguese and Hebrew but was never very good at speaking Dutch?

20. Which philosophy was founded by Zeno of Citium?

21. Which philosophical movement did Husserl found?

22. What common name is given to 'the theory of the conditions of valid inference'?

23. Which British philosopher, the godson of John Stuart Mill, was closely involved with the Campaign for Nuclear Disarmament?

24. Which movement emanated from the Vienna Circle?

25. Which philosophy takes the view that "man is the measure of all things"?

26. Which Spanish Jewish philosopher wrote *The Guide of the Perplexed*?

27. Which English mathematician gave his name to a recognized branch of algebra?

28. Who wrote the *Communist Manifesto*?

29. Which Frenchman is most frequently associated with 'deconstruction'?

30. Which philosophy holds that physical objects can have no existence apart from a mind that which is conscious of them?

SCORING

The maximum score is 30.

25–30
Brilliant! Your knowledge of the subject is first rate and sets you up for a career as a genius.

20–24
Very good. You have a superior knowledge of the subject and are at home with most of the important philosophical concepts.

15–19
Not bad, but you need to study more.

10–14
You are really not up to standard on this one. Try taking evening classes.

BELOW 10
You think Ethics is a place near London.

ANSWERS

1. Aristotle. 2. Peter Abelard. 3. Epistemology. 4. Ontology. 5. Descartes. 6. Ethics. 7. Kant. 8. Plato. 9. Hedonism. 10. Existentialism. 11. Dialectic. 12. Chomsky. 13. Cynicism. 14. Empiricism. 15. Hume. 16. Confucius. 17. Leibniz. 18. Locke. 19. Spinoza. 20. Stoicism. 21. Phenomenology. 22. Logic. 23. Russell. 24. Logical Positivism. 25. Relativism. 26. Maimonides. 27. Boole. 28. Marx. 29. Derrida. 30. Idealism.

SCIENCE

Today anyone with any hope of reaching the heights of genius must have some knowledge of science. You just can't decide "I'm an *artist* and don't know about that sort of thing" any more. Try your scientific knowledge with this test.

1. What does **DNA** stand for?

2. Which are the only cells of the human body that have no nucleus?

3. What does **LASER** stand for?

4. What is fission?

5. According to relativity, what happens to moving clocks?

6. What is a chaotic system?

7. What are the Four Forces in order of strength?

8. What do **GUT** and **TOE** stand for?

9. What substance causes the soreness in muscles used for heavy exercise?

10. Photosynthesis is the inverse of ———.

11. If you live in the **US**, how fast do the generators at your local power station turn?

12. What is another name for natural magnets, of the type made of iron?

13. What, according to relativity, happens to light passing near the sun?

14. Most of the mass of an atom, but almost none of its volume, lies in its ———.

15. Name the 'Oldest Human Ancestor', an australopithecine.

16. Name the Polish woman who was one of the founders of nuclear science.

17. What are the basic building blocks of carbohydrates?

18. The word 'cell' was first used in a biological sense by which English physicist?

19. How much of their **DNA** do humans share with other individuals?

20. What biological material was first seen by Antoine van Leeuwenhoek?

21. What temperature is normally considered to be absolute zero?

22. How close has anyone ever got to absolute zero in a laboratory?

124

23. How long ago did dinosaurs become extinct?

24. The gene for six fingers is dominant over the gene for five fingers. True or false?

25. The gene is the basic unit of what?

26. What is special about the bacteria known as Chlamydia and Rickettsia?

27. If someone dies after a fight or after being severely frightened, rigor mortis sets in more quickly. True or false?

28. Does helium come from the Earth's atmosphere?

29. What happens when electrical charges accelerate?

30. What can the human body detect that the human eye cannot?

ANSWERS

1. Deoxyribonucleic acid. 2. Red blood cells. 3. Light Amplification by Stimulated Emission of Radiation. 4. A process that splits a large nucleus into two or more smaller daughter nuclei. 5. They slow down. 6. One in which the final outcome depends very sensitively on the initial conditions. 7. Strong, Electromagnetic, Weak, Gravity. 8. The Grand Unified Theory, and the Theory of Everything. 9. Lactic acid. 10. Respiration. 11. 60 times per second (electrical current in the USA is rated at 60 Hertz). 12. Ferromagnets. 13. It gets bent. 14. Nucleus. 15. Lucy. 16. Marie Curie. 17. Sugars. 18. Robert Hooke. 19. 99.8% 20. Human sperm. 21. -273.17 degrees Celsius. 22. Within one billionth of a degree. 23. 65 million years. 24. True. 25. Heredity. 26. They are the smallest living things. 27. True. 28. No, it is found trapped with oil and natural gas. 29. Electromagnetic waves are produced. 30. Infrared radiation.

SCORING

The maximum score is 30.

25–30

You have a very profound knowledge of modern scientific thinking. This is clearly a field in which you feel quite at home and where you can exercise your abilities to the full.

20–24

You are well versed in much of modern science but still have much more to learn. This is clearly an area which you find fascinating and where you can make the most of your talent.

15–19

You have moderate scientific knowledge. As a background to some other field of activity this would be useful, but you are not equipped to make science your main occupation.

10–14

Science is not really for you. Try the other tests, there must be areas you find far more congenial.

BELOW 10

Your scientific knowledge could only be found with the aid of a rather powerful microscope.

ASSERTIVENESS

It seems unlikely that anyone would get recognized as a genius by being a shrinking violet. Most geniuses have been rather good at pushing themselves forward when it mattered. So let's test just how assertive you can be.

1. If someone pushes into line ahead of you, do you:

a) Harangue him in embarrassingly loud tones until he gives up.
b) Say, "Erm, sorry but I was here first."
c) Suffer in silence.

2. If you get poor service in a shop, do you:

a) Go home and write to the CEO of the company setting out your grievance in full.
b) Shout at the shop assistant.
c) Make bitter remarks to your fellow shoppers but fail to complain to the staff.

3. You take something to be mended and when you get it home the fault hasn't been fixed. Do you:

a) Phone the repair place and explain the problem.
b) Try to fix it yourself.
c) Storm back to the repair shop and demand to see the manager.

4. Whilst browsing in a bookshop you notice someone else's book full of your plagiarized ideas. Do you:

a) Take no notice, it might just be coincidence.
b) Consult a lawyer.
c) Contact the author to seek an explanation.

5. You try to attract attention in a crowded shop but don't get noticed. Do you:

a) Storm out in disgust.
b) Wait patiently until you get served.
c) Make a fuss until someone gives you attention.

6. You go for a job interview. Do you:

a) Explain confidently why you are the best person for the job.
b) Describe your qualifications and hope for the best.
c) Look at all the other candidates in the waiting room and wish you hadn't bothered.

7. Your child comes home and complains of having been picked on by her teacher. Do you:

a) Tell her to take no notice, it will all pass over.
b) Ask for an appointment with the teacher to sort the matter out.
c) Tell your child she has to stand up for herself.

8. Your neighbour regularly plays loud music late at night. Do you:

a) Call the police.
b) Go round and complain.
c) Improve your sound insulation.

9. **You get overlooked for promotion. Do you:**

a) Resign.

b) Complain to the boss that you deserved better.

c) Work hard to do better next time.

10. **You need a raise. Do you:**

a) Go straight to the boss and ask for one.

b) Take on extra work and hope that you get noticed.

c) Make some economies in your life style.

11. **You feel your boss does not appreciate your contribution to the company. Do you:**

a) Complain to your colleagues and hope he gets to hear about it.

b) Ask for a staff review.

c) Look through the 'situations vacant' ads.

12. **At a public meeting you find yourself in complete disagreement with the speaker. Do you:**

a) Leave the meeting.

b) Whisper your objections to the friend sitting beside you.

c) Stand up and ask pointed questions.

13. **Members of a religious sect with which you disagree come to your door. Do you:**

a) Tell them to go away.

b) Invite them in and set out your objections at length.

c) Make a financial contribution to get rid of them.

14. **Someone comes around collecting for charity. You already support a number of charities and cannot really afford to give more. Do you:**

a) Say that you're sorry but you have no change right now.

b) Explain honestly that you think you give enough.

c) Ignore the door bell and let them think you're out.

15. **A friend asks your opinion of some clothes s/he has just bought. Do you:**

a) Say honestly that they were not a good choice.

b) Change the subject.

c) Damn with faint praise and hope that the hint is taken.

16. **A political candidate comes to your door canvassing support in a forthcoming election. Do you:**

a) Tell him frankly that you won't be voting for him.

b) Say that you will vote for him (you have also said this to all the other candidates).

c) Discuss the issues and say that you will make up your mind later.

17. **Friends invite you to join them at a play you suspect will be boring. Do you:**

a) Go anyway and do your best to take an interest.

b) Point out that it's going to be dull and suggest doing something else.

c) Phone up at the last minute and say you're ill.

18. A person you find attractive makes some remarks with which you cannot agree. Do you:

a) Say nothing, you don't want to spoil your chances of a relationship.

b) Argue strongly for your own view and hope that honesty wins you Brownie points.

c) Remonstrate mildly but give up before you get into a real argument.

19. Is it more important to state your views clearly than to be popular?

a) Yes.

b) No.

c) Not sure.

20. Would you keep quiet on a subject you felt strongly about just to keep the peace?

a) Probably.

b) Certainly not.

c) Maybe.

21. Your mother-in-law arrives for the weekend and starts criticizing everything in your home. Do you:

a) Tell her that if she doesn't like it she can go straight home.

b) Take no notice, she'll be gone by Monday.

c) Quietly point out that your lifestyle suits you very well.

22. You find yourself at a sports match among a group of rival supporters. Do you:

a) Keep very quiet and hide your team colours.

b) Shout loudly for your team.

c) Joke with the rival supporters about being a member of the opposition.

23. A very large drunk in a bar is making obnoxious racist comments. Do you:

a) Leave the bar before trouble starts.

b) Try to start a discussion about the issues.

c) Tell him loudly that he's a bigot.

24. You see a police officer parking illegally to go and collect his dry cleaning. Do you:

a) Confront him and complain.

b) Ignore it, you don't want trouble with the police.

c) Write to his boss and make an official complaint.

25. At a PTA meeting you feel strongly that you should voice an unpopular point of view. Do you:

a) Say what you feel regardless of who you offend.

b) Keep quiet, you have to live with these people.

c) Write to the PTA Committee after the meeting stating your point of view.

SCORING

	1	2	3		1	2	3		1	2	3
1	c	b	a	10	c	b	a	19	b	c	a
2	c	b	a	11	c	a	b	20	a	c	b
3	b	a	c	12	a	b	c	21	b	c	a
4	a	b	c	13	c	a	b	22	a	c	b
5	a	b	c	14	c	a	b	23	a	b	c
6	c	b	a	15	b	c	a	24	b	c	a
7	a	c	b	16	b	c	a	25	b	c	a
8	c	a	b	17	c	a	b				
9	a	c	b	18	a	c	b				

SCORING

The maximum score is 75.

70–75

Yes, you're very assertive and will have no trouble getting people to take notice of what you say. It doesn't make you a genius but, if you've got what it takes, then at least you won't be ignored. You probably upset people by being so forthright but, if you want to make it in the genius league, you can't afford to let that kind of thing worry you or change your mind. And you don't.

60–69

You're quite assertive and do not usually have trouble getting your point across. However, to be accepted as a genius you may need to be even more forceful. The genius business is a tough one to break into and you'll need all the assertiveness you can muster.

40–59

No. You're too nice. Either toughen up or forget any dreams of genius. No one is going to take you seriously.

BELOW 40

You're joking, right?

ARROGANCE

This one is going to be a trifle difficult. The problem is that if you're going to be a genius you probably need to be arrogant. Very arrogant. It's hard to imagine someone self-effacing making it in the high-flying world of genius. We've already tested assertiveness and that was all right because no one really minds being called assertive. Even 'bossy' is not too bad. But arrogant? Oh dear. Let's see how you get on.

1. **'If you don't like it you can lump it!' Is this something you would say?**
   a) No, that's incredibly rude.
   b) Why not? You have to show people where they stand.
   c) I might if I was provoked enough.

2. **'The bigger they come the harder they fall.' Do you believe this?**
   a) That's right. Hit 'em hard so they don't get up.
   b) Erm, it's usually a case of, 'The bigger they come the harder I fall.'
   c) Yes, that's right. In theory at least.

3. **'You don't have to agree with me as long as you do as I say.' Would you agree with this?**
   a) It's sometimes necessary to be forceful.
   b) That is just *so* arrogant.
   c) Yes, you have to show people where they stand. Or kneel, preferably.

4. **'I always like to listen to the other person's point of view.' Is this a policy you endorse?**
   a) Why?
   b) Yes, if I have the time.
   c) Of course, I would always do it.

5. **'It is far better to reach a mutually satisfactory agreement than to force someone to admit defeat.' Your reaction?**
   a) Of course, that's the way it should be.
   b) If you can make that work, then fine. Otherwise you have to use force.
   c) No, you just stamp and shout until you get your own way.

6. **'I'd make a wonderful diplomat.' Would you?**
   a) No, I'd start World War 3.
   b) Yes, I'm very good at diplomacy.
   c) I'm quite diplomatic.

7. **Do you feel it necessary to consult other people and take notice of their opinions?**
   a) It's often very valuable.
   b) Why should I? What do they know?
   c) It can be useful sometimes.

8. **Barefaced cheek gets you a long way in life. Do you agree?**
   a) Yes, it seldom fails.
   b) I wouldn't know, I've never tried.
   c) It's not a tactic I use often, but it has worked occasionally.

9. 'People listen to me because I'm always right.' Agree?

a) No, I don't like that at all.

b) No, I'm right sometimes but I wouldn't claim to be infallible.

c) Call me arrogant if you like but that's the way it is.

10. 'I think that a certain amount of modesty is essential for a well-rounded character.' What do you think.

a) Who wants to be 'well rounded'? If you've got it flaunt it!

b) I think modesty is very important.

c) Modesty is OK, but you can overdo it.

11. 'When driving I expect others to get out of my way.' Agree?

a) I try to play fair with other road users.

b) My time is important, OK? I don't need people slowing me down.

c) Sometimes I'm in a hurry and need to push ahead, but I try not to.

12. 'I'm embarrassed if people defer to me.' Does this seem familiar?

a) I'm furious if they don't.

b) Yes, that's what I'm like.

c) I can empathize with that, though I try not to be too self-effacing.

13. 'I expect people to admire my achievements.' Do you?

a) No, not really.

b) It would be nice if they recognized my worth.

c) They'll regret it if they don't!

14. 'I am not one of the common herd.' Does that describe you?

a) I wouldn't put it quite like that, though I do think I have great ability.

b) Good gracious no!

c) Of course it describes me. Who else?

15. 'I have nothing to declare except my genius.' Would you agree with Oscar Wilde?

a) No, of course not.

b) Not really, though I do have great talent.

c) Yes, of course. Who's Oscar Wilde?

16. 'My work is of the utmost importance to mankind.' Is yours?

a) Naturally.

b) No, not at all.

c) It's quite important but not vital.

17. 'My name will go down in history.' Will yours?

a) No.

b) I would like to think so, but I'm not sure.

c) Of course.

18. 'People are unable to understand my true greatness.' Agree?

a) Yes, but the loss is theirs.

b) No, that's rubbish.

c) I'm good but I'm not *that* good.

19. 'My family has to revolve around me.' Agree?

a) I usually try to fit in but sometimes my needs have to come first.

b) I always consider others.

c) Yes, just like the Solar System.

20. 'I enjoy the limelight.' Do you?

a) Not at all.

b) It's nice for a change.

c) Enjoy? Try 'demand'.

21. 'I deserve the admiration and respect of others.' Do you?

a) Yes, I suppose so.

b) No, I wouldn't say that.

c) Yes, and I'd better get it, too.

22. 'There are only a couple of hundred people who really run things in this country, and I'm one of them.' Are you?

a) I don't think that's true and, even if it is, it certainly doesn't include me.

b) I'm influential, but not that influential.

c) Yes, that's the way things work.

23. 'People recognize me wherever I go.' Is this you?

a) Yes, I'm used to it.

b) Some people know me if they read my work.

c) No, I'm not at all famous.

24. 'When I go anywhere I expect to be treated like a VIP.' Do you?

a) No, I'd hate that.

b) Yes, I'd accept nothing less.

c) On some occasions.

25. 'Other people only exist to make my life easier.' Do you agree?

a) Of course, a genius has to be pampered.

b) That is just so ugly.

c) Maybe, to some extent.

SCORING

	1	2	3		1	2	3		1	2	3
1	a	c	b	10	b	c	a	19	b	a	c
2	b	c	a	11	a	c	b	20	a	b	c
3	b	a	c	12	b	c	a	21	b	a	c
4	c	b	a	13	a	b	c	22	a	b	c
5	a	b	c	14	b	a	c	23	c	b	a
6	b	c	a	15	a	b	c	24	a	c	b
7	a	c	b	16	b	c	a	25	b	c	a
8	b	c	a	17	a	b	c				
9	a	b	c	18	b	c	a				

SCORING

The maximum score is 75.

70–75

Your arrogance is such that you won't even be reading this. You know how great you are.

60–69

Genius is within your reach on this score. You are pretty arrogant, but not so bad that you can't see the offence you give.

40–59

You don't really understand arrogance that well. You have too much of a conscience ever to be really arrogant.

BELOW 40

You're far too pleasant for the genius game. Congratulations!

CHARISMA

If you're going to be a genius you will need charisma, that magnetic power that attracts people to you. Why? It won't affect the quality of your work or provide you with wonderful, original ideas but, as we've seen in the introductory chapters, a large part of being a genius is making people *believe* that you are one. If people who don't even understand what you're talking about believe that you are in fact a genius, you will have made it. The following test will decide whether you've got what it takes.

1. Do people find themselves attracted to you?

a) Yes, it can be embarrassing sometimes.

b) No, no more than other people.

c) I suppose they do a bit.

2. Do you find that people agree with you regardless of the quality of your arguments?

a) No, never.

b) Not that often.

c) All the time.

3. Would you make a good political leader?

a) Yes, people would vote for me no matter what my policies were.

b) No, with the best policies in the world I couldn't get elected.

c) I'd be average.

4. Would you find it easy to attract followers?

a) No, not at all.

b) Not very easy.

c) Yes, it's really no problem.

5. Do you find casual acquaintances open up and tell you their life story in intimate detail?

a) Occasionally.

b) Never.

c) Happens all the time. Sometimes I just can't get away.

6. Do children and animals take to you immediately?

a) They usually bite me.

b) I get on with them OK, I suppose.

c) Yes, I'm always popular with kids and pets.

7. Do strangers choose to sit next to you on the train?

a) Frequently.

b) Sometimes.

c) As little as possible.

8. Do people come up to you in the street and ask directions?

a) Not often.

b) Sometimes.

c) Very often.

9. Do you ever feel that people avoid you for no obvious reason?

a) Yes, it's unpleasant and I don't understand it.

b) It has happened very occasionally.

c) No, that never happens to me.

10. Does your work attract disciples?

a) Yes, frequently.

b) Not at all.

c) I suppose a few.

11. Could you sway a crowd just by force of personality?

a) I have done many times.

b) No, I'd need more than that.

c) I could influence them a bit, but not make them storm the Bastille, for example.

12. Do people customarily look to you for leadership?

a) From time to time.

b) Absolutely never.

c) Very frequently.

13. Do old friends keep in touch with you even though there is no practical advantage to them?

a) Yes, I still have friends from the distant past.

b) No, gone and forgotten, that's me.

c) I have some old friends.

14. Do people tend to fall in love with you?

a) No more than usually, I guess.

b) Yes, it happens all the time. I'm used to it.

c) No, that isn't really my problem. Worse luck.

15. Do people tend to be possessive over you?

a) No, never.

b) Not often.

c) Yes, it can be a real problem.

16. Do you feel that you have some sort of supernormal power over people?

a) I might do sometimes.

b) No, not at all.

c) Yes, I have suspected it.

17. Could you face down an angry mob?

a) I'd try but wouldn't guarantee the result.

b) I'd get lynched.

c) I could do it.

18. Would people accept an unusual idea just because you proposed it?

a) Possibly.

b) No, the fact that it was mine would make things more difficult.

c) Yes, that would be enough.

19. Do you find it easy to take the lead in public discussions?

a) Not at all.

b) Yes, I do it all the time.

c) Sometimes.

20. Are you good at being a follower?

a) No, I always lead.

b) Yes, it suits my personality.

c) I can be follower or leader according to the situation.

21. Do you get frightened if people make demands of you?

a) No, I'm used to it.

b) It disturbs me slightly.

c) I find it quite alarming.

22. If you weren't going to be a genius, would you have considered a career as a popular entertainer?

a) I'd hate every minute of it.

b) The thought does attract me.

c) I'm not sure. I might like it.

23. Do you find the attention of others stimulating?

a) Yes, of course.

b) No, it embarrasses me.

c) I'm so used to it I hardly notice any more, but I suppose I would miss it.

24. Regardless of your actual religious beliefs, do you have the skill to be a preacher?

a) Oh yes, nothing would be easier.

b) I could, but I don't know how successful I'd be.

c) No, I'd have an empty church.

25. Could you sell things just by the force of your personality?

a) No, not at all.

b) I might do quite well.

c) No problem at all. People always want to please me.

SCORING

	1	2	3		1	2	3		1	2	3
1	b	c	a	10	b	c	a	19	a	c	b
2	a	b	c	11	b	c	a	20	b	c	a
3	b	c	a	12	b	a	c	21	c	b	a
4	a	b	c	13	b	c	a	22	a	c	b
5	b	a	c	14	c	a	b	23	b	a	c
6	a	b	c	15	a	b	c	24	c	b	a
7	c	b	a	16	b	a	c	25	a	b	c
8	a	b	c	17	b	a	c				
9	a	b	c	18	b	a	c				

SCORING

The maximum score is 75.

70–75

You have massive charisma. Your influence over others, for good or ill, is very strong.

60–69

You are quite charismatic and could easily convince people of your genius. You have a considerable influence.

40–59

People find you likeable. They will listen patiently to your ideas but, in the end, will make up their minds according to the facts.

BELOW 40

Charisma is not really your strong suit, is it?

CONCEPTUAL THINKING

To be a genius, you need to think conceptually. On the whole geniuses are not nuts and bolts kind of people. They see the big picture and they work with ideas rather than practicalities. See how you shape up as a conceptual thinker in this test.

1. Would you rather understand the principles by which your central heating system works, or be able to fix it when it goes wrong?
a) I don't really care as long as it works.
b) I would want to understand all about it.
c) I'm happy to be able to fix it, but I don't care about the theory.

2. Can you repair a car engine?
a) Wouldn't have a clue!
b) Yes, that's no problem.
c) I'd try, but wouldn't guarantee the result.

3. Do you toy with ideas just for the fun of it?
a) Yes, all the time.
b) No, there's no point to it.
c) Yes, some ideas intrigue me.

4. Do you like to tinker with machinery?
a) I don't mind.
b) I couldn't be bothered.
c) I'm never happier than when playing with machines.

5. Are you really into DIY?
a) Not at all.
b) Only when my partner nags me.
c) Yes, I find it very satisfying.

6. Do you enjoy mathematics?
a) Yes, I'm fascinated by it.
b) No, it bores me.
c) I'm quite interested.

7. Can you understand music theory?
a) Not at all.
b) Yes, of course.
c) I did a bit at school.

8. Do you play chess?
a) Yes, I'm very keen when I get the time.
b) I can play but don't often bother.
c) No, I never mastered it.

9. Would you rather fix a broken machine or go to a concert?
a) I'd quite enjoy either.
b) Give me the machine any day.
c) I'd rather go to the dentist than fix a machine!

10. Do you itch to know how things work?
a) Yes, I'm full of curiosity.
b) No, as long as they work that's fine by me.
c) I'm quite interested but not obsessed.

11. **Do you ache to understand why things work?**

a) Yes, that's more like it!

b) Yes, that's quite interesting.

c) No, couldn't care less.

12. **Would you learn a new language even if you had no chance to use it?**

a) What for?

b) I might.

c) Yes, there are all sorts of languages I'd love to learn but none of them is that useful.

13. **Would you rather theorize about the universe or help build a space rocket?**

a) I'd enjoy both.

b) The rocket sounds fun.

c) I enjoy theorizing.

14. **Do your friends regard you as a little impractical?**

a) I suppose they do.

b) That's the last thing anyone would say about me.

c) No, I don't think so.

15. **Does everyone turn to you when machines break down?**

a) Always.

b) Not unless they want them broken a bit more!

c) Mending machines is not what I do best.

16. **Can you programme the video (VCR)?**

a) Yes, can't everyone?

b) I sometimes get it wrong.

c) The damn thing hates me!

17. **Do you just pay people to sort out the practical aspects of your life?**

a) I wouldn't have put it quite so bluntly, but yes.

b) There are some things I just can't do myself.

c) No. I'd never need that sort of help.

18. **Do you find philosophy intriguing?**

a) Not in the slightest.

b) I'm fairly interested.

c) Yes, I'd love to devote more time to it.

19. **Do you see academic research as out of touch with reality?**

a) Not really.

b) Yes, academics give me a pain.

c) No, of course not. Research is *about* reality.

20. **Do you take pride in your ability to make machines work?**

a) Yes, I do.

b) No, it would be misplaced pride in my case.

c) Machines are in a conspiracy against me.

21. **Do you take pride in not knowing how machines work?**

a) Yes, I hate them as much as they hate me.

b) No, I can't stand people like that.

c) No, ignorance is never something to be proud of.

22. **Can you drive a car?**

a) Yes, I'm an excellent driver.

b) Yes, like most people I guess.

c) No, I've never bothered to learn.

23. If the written language of the Philistines were discovered tomorrow, would you be excited?

a) That would be incredible!

b) Why would I care about some dead Philistines?

c) Interesting, but not that interesting.

24. Do you think much about the meaning of life?

a) Sometimes.

b) No, I'm too busy.

c) Yes, of course, it's the most important question there is.

25. Would you like to be in charge of, say, the engine room of an aircraft carrier?

a) Can you afford to lose the ship?

b) No, not quite me.

c) Yes, just give me the chance!

SCORING

	1	2	3		1	2	3		1	2	3
1	b	c	a	10	a	c	b	19	b	a	c
2	b	c	a	11	c	b	a	20	a	b	c
3	b	c	a	12	a	b	c	21	b	c	a
4	c	a	b	13	b	a	c	22	a	b	c
5	c	b	a	14	b	c	a	23	b	c	a
6	b	c	a	15	a	c	b	24	b	a	c
7	a	c	b	16	a	b	c	25	c	b	a
8	c	b	a	17	c	b	a				
9	b	a	c	18	a	b	c				

SCORING

The maximum score is 75.

70–75

You are almost entirely conceptual in your thinking. You don't have a practical bone in your body and you don't care. Your life is spent wrestling with abstract concepts which you find completely fascinating and you let others take care of the practicalities. You have definite genius potential as long as you don't trip over your untied shoelaces and break your neck first.

60–69

You are strongly conceptual in your thinking but not entirely unaware of the practicalities of life. You could not only design an experiment but could probably make it work. OK, you could tell *someone else* how to make it work. Your genius potential is quite high but, if it doesn't work out, your chances of a job in a garage are not good.

40–59

You're far too practical to be a genius. You can mend fuses and, probably, program the video.

BELOW 40

You wouldn't know a concept if you found one in your lunch. By the way, you just got grease marks all over this book!

CONTROL

To be a genius you need to be fully in control of your life. More than that: you need to *believe* you are in control. Are you the sort of person who is master of his fate, or do you believe that your life is controlled from outside? This test will help you find that out.

1. Are you fully confident of the course your life is taking?

a) It's taking the course I want, naturally.

b) I worry about it sometimes.

c) I have no idea where my life is going.

2. Do you feel that you are in the 'driving seat' of your life?

a) No, I think I'm more of a passenger.

b) Yes, I'm mostly in control.

c) Yes, and I don't allow back seat drivers either!

3. Do you believe in fate?

a) I suppose so.

b) Yes, I believe very strongly that some things are pre-ordained.

c) No, I've no patience with rubbish like that.

4. Do you make your own luck?

a) No, I think luck comes from elsewhere.

b) Yes, you have to.

c) I try to help myself as best I can.

5. Would you like to captain an ocean-going liner?

a) I'd be terrified.

b) I'd love the challenge.

c) I'd like to but I'm not sure that I could.

6. What do you think of the saying, 'You can't fight city hall'?

a) Nonsense, you can fight anyone.

b) It's probably true.

c) You can always fight, but you may not win.

7. Do you wear the pants in your family?

a) No, my partner does.

b) We all get along just fine without power games.

c) Yes, of course.

8. What are you like as a subordinate?

a) Dreadful, I always know best.

b) I don't mind taking orders at all.

c) I'm OK but I sometimes question decisions.

9. Do you like team games?

a) Yes, I enjoy the camaraderie.

b) I don't mind, but I'm not that keen.

c) Only if I get to be captain.

10. Do you fear responsibility?

a) A bit.

b) It can be quite frightening to be in charge.

c) I need the feeling of being in control.

11. Do you tend to blame society for juvenile delinquency?
a) To a certain extent.
b) Yes, I think young people are led astray by society's lack of values.
c) People are responsible for themselves. No one makes you become a criminal.

12. Would you like to be self-employed?
a) No, it would be too risky.
b) I wouldn't mind, but it would be scary.
c) I couldn't work any other way.

13. Would you like to be part of a community, like the army, for example?
a) Yes, I like the thought of other people taking some of the responsibility.
b) No, I can't stand all that 'team spirit' stuff.
c) I wouldn't mind too much

14. Do you think people should have total responsibility for their own lives?
a) That seems rather harsh to me.
b) Maybe, but a little help is sometimes needed.
c) Yes, how could you live any other way?

15. Do you hate giving up control when you are ill?
a) It drives me mad.
b) No, I quite enjoy the rest from responsibility.
c) I don't mind letting go for a while.

16. Do you sometimes feel that life is against you?
a) Not really.
b) Yes, I often feel that way.
c) Couldn't care less, I'm in charge of my life.

17. Do you believe we have free will?
a) I'm not sure.
b) No I don't think we do.
c) I know I do.

18. Do you ever read your horoscope?
a) Yes, just for fun.
b) I take it quite seriously.
c) What a load of rubbish!

19. Is the course of your life pre-determined?
a) Of course not.
b) It might be.
c) Yes, I think there are things we cannot change.

20. Do you ever feel in need of divine help?
a) All the time.
b) I believe God does help us.
c) No, I can make it on my own, thank you.

21. Do you have complete faith in yourself?
a) Yes, who else should I have it in?
b) Mostly.
c) No, quite often I doubt myself.

22. Are you certain that you are in control of your life?
a) Quite certain.
b) I like to think so.
c) I'm not at all sure.

23. Do you have faith in the power of the Government to control your life?
a) What, a crowd of sleazy politicians? I certainly don't need *them*.
b) Yes, of course, after all we elected them.
c) On the whole I'm happy to let them be in control.

140

24. Do you always know best?

a) About my own life, certainly.

b) I'm open to advice.

c) I often need someone to tell me what to do.

25. Are you the captain of your ship?

a) Yes, and I don't stand for any mutinies either!

b) Most of the time.

c) No, someone else seems to run my ship

SCORING

	1	2	3			1	2	3			1	2	3			1	2	3
1	c	b	a		8	b	c	a		15	b	c	a		22	c	b	a
2	a	b	c		9	a	b	c		16	b	a	c		23	b	c	a
3	b	a	c		10	b	a	c		17	b	a	c		24	c	b	a
4	a	c	b		11	b	a	c		18	b	a	c		25	c	b	a
5	a	c	b		12	a	b	c		19	c	b	a					
6	b	c	a		13	a	c	b		20	a	b	c					
7	a	b	c		14	a	b	c		21	c	b	a					

SCORING

The maximum score is 75.

70–75

You are very self-directed and this will stand you in good stead in your quest to become a genius. Other people may find you rather distant and a bit bossy but, on the other hand, there will be plenty of time when they are grateful to you for taking charge. Either way you won't care much, you'll just get on with knowing best.

60–69

You are quite firmly in charge of your own life. You have no truck with luck, fate, or the Government when it comes to knowing what is best for you. But you are aware that you can't always be in charge however much you might want to be.

40–59

You don't really understand about being in control of your life. You are far too dependent on outside help to ever make it in the genius league.

BELOW 40

Your life appears to be controlled from another planet. Possibly another galaxy.

DEFERRED GRATIFICATION

What exactly is 'deferred gratification?', you might well ask. (Though if you want to be considered a genius you need to *know* this kind of stuff.) OK, imagine you're a toddler and someone says to you, "I'll give you a marshmallow. You can eat it right away if you want. But in a moment I'm going to leave the room and if, when I come back, you *haven't* eaten your marshmallow, I'll give you two more." What would you do? Why does it matter? Well, a psychologist tried this experiment with some kids and got an interesting result. Kids who showed they were capable of deferred gratification – ie, those who could wait in order to gain an advantage – did much better in later life than those who ate the marshmallow straight away. So, if you want to be a genius, then a capacity for deferred gratification would be highly desirable. Can you do it? Try this test to find out.

1. **Let's start with the marshmallow. Could you wait, say, 20 minutes in order to get two more marshmallows? Be honest!**
a) Yes, I could wait twice that long if I had to.
b) No, I'd give in and eat the one in my hand.
c) I'd probably be able to wait but it would be a very close thing.

2. **Do you sneak a look at presents?**
a) I have done.
b) No, that would spoil the surprise.
c) I always do, I just can't help it.

3. **Do you often say, 'I can't *wait!*' and actually mean it?**
a) Never.
b) Oh, yes!
c) Not often, but sometimes.

4. **Would you plant a tree that was slow growing, an oak, say?**
a) I might do.
b) Of course, it would be my gift to the future.
c) Why? What would be the point?

5. **Would you save up for an expensive holiday that you couldn't go on for five years, or would you rather go on cheaper holidays now?**
a) I'd take the cheaper holidays. Who knows how long you're going to live?
b) I would consider saving up.
c) I'd definitely save.

6. **Do you sneak food from the kitchen when a meal is being prepared?**
a) No, I've never done such a thing.
b) Yes, sometimes I can't resist.
c) Of course, doesn't everyone?

7. Does waiting for something good to happen frustrate you?

a) No, I rather enjoy the anticipation.

b) I scream with frustration.

c) I don't mind too much, as long as I don't wait long.

8. You finish a good book and want to get the sequel from the library. Someone's got it out on loan. What do you do?

a) Rush to the book store and buy a copy.

b) Reserve the book and wait until it comes back into circulation.

c) Wait with growing impatience.

9. You want to buy some new clothes. The shop you normally go to is out of stock but will have what you want by next week. Their other branch, 50 miles away, has just what you want right now. Do you:

a) Wait until your local branch has what you want.

b) Jump in the car and drive the 50 miles.

c) Call the other branch to see if they will let you order by phone.

10. Do you find waiting for something you want comes easily to you?

a) To be honest it doesn't come to me at all.

b) I don't mind waiting a bit.

c) I never mind waiting, the result is usually worth it.

11. You're waiting to see the latest movie. There's an announcement that the projector has broken down and it will take half an hour to get it fixed. Do you:

a) Go out and get a pizza, then come back in half an hour.

b) Wait uncomplainingly for the fault to be fixed.

c) Complain strongly to the manager, then spend the half hour in a filthy temper.

12. You or your partner is expecting a baby. You *could* find out what sex it is going to be. Do you?

a) Yes, I couldn't bear not to know.

b) I might, depending on what my partner wanted.

c) I would wait. Knowing would spoil the surprise, wouldn't it?

13. You take an exam but then go on holiday abroad. The results will be sent to you by mail. Eventually. Do you:

a) Hang around foreign post offices waiting for a message.

b) Make a very expensive phone call to find out.

c) Wait until you get back to find out.

14. You're sent away on business which involves you being separated from your partner/lover. What do you do?

a) Get the job done as quickly as possible and go home.

b) Phone, write, email, rush through the job and catch the first flight back.

c) Take your time and do the work thoroughly. A break will do you both good.

15. How long could you wait for something you *really* wanted?

a) Given a choice, seconds.

b) Certainly hours or days, weeks or months would be a problem.

c) Years, if necessary.

16. Do you think that patience is a virtue?

a) Yes, and one that I possess.

b) No, but I'm quite patient.

c) No, I hate patience. Why should I be patient?!

17. Do you have a pension?

a) What for? I mean, I'm not going to retire for years.

b) Of course, it is better to be prudent.

c) Yes, though I don't pay as much into it as I should.

18. Would you devote yourself to a long-term project, such as scientific research, that might not pay off for many years, if at all?

a) I might if the work was sufficiently interesting.

b) Life's too short.

c) I certainly would. Anything worth doing takes time.

19. A mysterious present arrives unexpectedly. However, you have an urgent appointment to attend. What do you do?

a) Rip the paper off, open the present and forget about the appointment.

b) Leave the tempting parcel until you get back. Anticipation is half the pleasure.

c) Go to the appointment and get away as quickly as possible to get to your surprise.

20. You are offered a new job with more pay. However, if you stay where you are your prospects within three years are excellent. What do you do?

a) Go, you've had enough of this place anyway.

b) Stay, the rewards of patience may be rich.

c) Hang on a bit longer, but still look out for other offers.

21. 'Everything comes to he who waits' Agree?

a) I suppose quite often that's true.

b) I think that is only common sense.

c) No. You have to go out and grab what you want.

22. Could you work in a job where promotion is by the 'dead men's shoes' method?

a) Yes, it wouldn't bother me.

b) If I did, some people would be dead sooner than expected!

c) I suppose I could, but I'd get very frustrated.

23. At the end of next week you're going to be given a huge honour which will be televised nationally. How do you feel?

a) Can't wait!

b) It'll be nice when it happens.

c) A bit nervous but otherwise OK.

24. You want to go to a sports match but first you need to do some household chores. Do you:

a) Forget the chores and slide out of the house unnoticed.

b) Do your chores conscientiously.

c) Rush to get the work done so that you can get away sooner.

25. You stand to inherit a lot of money from a distant relative. Do you:

a) Forget about it. The money will come eventually.

b) Think about it sometimes with longing.

c) Wish ardently that the relative would go to his reward. After all, it's not as if he's anyone close...

SCORING

	1	2	3			1	2	3			1	2	3			1	2	3
1	b	c	a		**8**	a	c	b		**15**	a	b	c		**22**	b	c	a
2	c	a	b		**9**	b	c	a		**16**	c	b	a		**23**	a	c	b
3	b	c	a		**10**	a	b	c		**17**	a	c	b		**24**	a	c	b
4	c	a	b		**11**	c	a	b		**18**	b	a	c		**25**	c	b	a
5	a	b	c		**12**	a	b	c		**19**	a	c	b					
6	c	b	a		**13**	b	a	c		**20**	a	c	b					
7	b	c	a		**14**	b	a	c		**21**	c	a	b					

SCORING

The maximum score is 75.

70–75

You have no problem with deferred gratification, you could win prizes at it. You can wait forever for anything that you really want and nothing will put you off.

60–69

You don't have much of a problem with waiting but there are some limits to your patience. Still, you can hold out long enough to qualify for genius status.

40–59

You are not really exceptional in this department. In fact you have a decided tendency to impatience when a more considered attitude would be of help. Try to relax and let good things happen to you.

BELOW 40

Don't go, you haven't even got your result yet!

DETERMINATION

To become a genius requires considerable determination. You will encounter innumerable difficulties and will have to overcome them all. Try this test to see how you will get on.

1. Do you take 'no' for an answer?
a) Not if I can help it.
b) Yes, often you have no choice but to admit defeat.
c) I try not to, but sometimes it is inevitable.

2. Do you have a clear idea of where you are going in life?
a) Of course, I think about it all the time.
b) No, I don't give it much consideration.
c) Yes, I think I do.

3. Do you always achieve your ambitions?
a) Only sometimes.
b) Yes, I never fail.
c) No, usually I mess up.

4. Do feel that your problems are usually solvable?
a) Yes, there is always a way.
b) Usually there's a solution.
c) Some problems just cannot be solved.

5. Have you ever felt like giving up on life?
a) Never, it's not my style.
b) Sometimes things get just too much.
c) Yes, I feel that way most of the time.

6. Do you let anyone get in the way of what you want to do?
a) I suppose so, sometimes.
b) No, it would never even cross my mind.
c) Happens to me all the time.

7. Does criticism deter you from your chosen path?
a) Not at all.
b) Occasionally.
c) Yes, I find it puts me off quite a lot.

8. Are you ambitious?
a) Not at all.
b) Moderately.
c) Yes, ambition is very important to my life.

9. Do you have a clear idea of what you want to achieve?
a) No not really.
b) I've got some idea, but I keep changing my mind.
c) Yes, I'm totally focused.

10. If necessary would you take some menial job in order to finance your real plans?
a) No, I don't think I could do that.
b) Yes, of course I would.
c) I might, but I wouldn't like it much.

11. Do you suffer fools gladly?
a) Yes, I'm really very patient.
b) Sometimes, but I try not to.
c) No, I tell them where to go.

12. Do you regard your work as far more important than the problems of others?

a) No, I think that would be arrogant.

b) Yes, I do sometimes.

c) You're damn right I do.

13. Could you ever contemplate giving up your plans and doing something less demanding?

a) I suppose I might.

b) Yes, I've certainly thought about it.

c) I'd rather die.

14. If you were to become seriously ill, would you still struggle to complete your work?

a) Yes, to my last breath.

b) No, I'd rather spend time with my family.

c) I might, but it depends on other factors.

15. Would you let family and friends come between you and your work?

a) Never, in any circumstances.

b) Yes, to a certain extent.

c) Yes, I'm very family-minded.

16. Would you make any personal sacrifice to complete the task you have set yourself?

a) No, I suppose not.

b) Yes, but there must be limits.

c) I'd do anything that it takes.

17. Are you at all influenced by issues such as personal comfort?

a) No, that never enters my head.

b) Yes, I need to be comfortable to work well.

c) I need moderate comfort but I can rough it when I need to.

18. Would you willingly go without sleep on a regular basis to further your work?

a) No, I couldn't do that.

b) Yes, it would be a very small sacrifice to make.

c) I might do, for a short while.

19. On a scale of 1-10, how hard driving would you say you are (1 = easy going, 10 = completely remorseless)

a) 1 – 3.

b) 4 – 7.

c) 8 – 10.

20. Do you think others regard you as a determined person?

a) Certainly.

b) Maybe.

c) Probably not.

21. Do you make your work occupy most of your waking life?

a) Yes, I rarely think of anything else.

b) I work a lot, but not all the time.

c) No, I don't work that much really.

22. On a scale of 1-10, how important is your work to you. (1 = Not very important at all, 10 = Almost as important as breathing.)

a) 1 – 3.

b) 4 – 7.

c) 8 – 10.

23. Do you get upset by the petty frustrations of life?

a) Yes, they drive me crazy.

b) Sometimes I get quite annoyed.

c) No, they really don't worry me that much.

24. Do you expect others to make allowances for the importance of your work?

a) No, of course not.

b) Yes, I most certainly do.

c) Sometimes it's necessary.

25. Do you feel that other people's problems take up your valuable time?

a) Yes, and it infuriates me.

b) No, I never mind.

c) It can be a pest if I'm busy.

SCORING

	1	2	3		1	2	3		1	2	3		1	2	3
1	b	c	a	8	a	b	c	15	c	b	a	22	a	b	c
2	b	c	a	9	a	b	c	16	a	b	c	23	c	b	a
3	c	a	b	10	a	c	b	17	b	c	a	24	a	c	b
4	c	b	a	11	a	b	c	18	a	c	b	25	b	c	a
5	c	b	a	12	a	b	c	19	a	b	c				
6	c	a	b	13	b	a	c	20	c	b	a				
7	c	b	a	14	b	c	a	21	c	b	a				

SCORING

The maximum score is 75.

70–75

You're so determined it's frightening. You show a ruthlessness that may well help you to succeed but will leave you with few friends. Then again, when has a genius needed friends? To you your work is everything.

60–69

You are determined and push yourself hard. You are not quite blind to things outside of work but find it hard to make time for them.

40–59

You are quite hard-driving but also appreciate the necessity of making room for others in your life. There is a softer side to your nature which people will find attractive. However, you may not have the push needed to scale the heights of genius.

BELOW 40

You aren't taking this seriously, are you? Put your feet up! Have a good time! A genius you're not.

ENTHUSIASM

In order to become a genius you will need huge amounts of enthusiasm. You can't expect to scale the heights of mental achievement if you are half-hearted. The following test aims to see just how enthusiastic you are. It takes a broad view of the subject because, at the end of the day, it will be your attitude to life, and not just to your own subject, that will make the difference.

1. Do you greet each new day with pleasurable anticipation?

a) Yes, that's me.

b) No, I wake up feeling like hell.

c) Depends on the day, doesn't it?

2. Do you look forward to challenges yet to come?

a) No, I'd rather stay unchallenged if you don't mind.

b) I take it as it comes.

c) Yes, I enjoy a challenge.

3. Do you fear problems or view them as challenges?

a) Problems are just challenges in disguise.

b) My problems are just problems.

c) I know what you mean, but even so problems give me trouble.

4. What do you think of the proposition, 'Life's a bitch and then you die'.

a) No, that's cynical and defeatist.

b) Yes, that just about sums it up.

c) No, I don't feel that bad about it, though I do get discouraged.

5. Do you constantly seek new projects to throw yourself into?

a) No, I have enough problems with what I do already.

b) Yes, within reason.

c) Of course! There just aren't enough hours in the day for me.

6. Do you feel you love your work?

a) Yes, it is the best bit of my life.

b) No, I hate the sight of it most of the time.

c) 'Love' would be too strong a word; 'like' I could cope with.

7. Do you get excited when you come to understand a new concept?

a) Not at all.

b) Yes, from time to time.

c) That's the sort of thing that gives me a real buzz.

8. Is enthusiasm necessary for you to perform at your best?

a) I couldn't live a day without it.

b) It would be nice.

c) No, I have to get on with it however I feel.

9. **Do you tend to be the one who jollies people into doing things about which they may feel unenthusiastic?**

a) Yes, that's usually my job. People can be so grouchy.

b) No, I'd only make them feel worse.

c) Yes, sometimes I can be the enthusiastic one.

10. **Do you take on extra work just because you enjoy doing it?**

a) No, I have enough to do already.

b) Perhaps.

c) Yes, of course. I told you I *enjoy* my work!

11. **Do you feel that life is to be lived to the full?**

a) That's always been my philosophy.

b) No, I don't have time.

c) Yes, I try to feel that way, though sometimes it's difficult.

12. **Do you sometimes just 'run out of steam'?**

a) Yes, doesn't everyone?

b) Not too often.

c) No, why would I?

13. **Do you ever feel that your work has become too routine?**

a) Occasionally.

b) Yes, that's *just* how I feel.

c) No, of course not.

14. **Do you sometimes get the impression that you have to run faster just to remain in the same place?**

a) No, I never feel that way.

b) Yes, it can seem like that sometimes.

c) Yes, it seems more like that every day.

15. **Do people look to you for encouragement when things get tough?**

a) It has happened.

b) No, they'd be looking in the wrong place.

c) That's one of my good points.

16. **'Life is just a bowl of cherries.' How do you feel about this statement?**

a) It may sound silly, but it's true.

b) It's as dumb as it sounds.

c) It may be true sometimes, but not always.

17. **Do you always feel as if you are firing on all cylinders?**

a) No I don't.

b) Yes, all the time.

c) Mostly.

18. **Do you do get easily discouraged?**

a) Never.

b) I suppose I do from time to time.

c) Yes, it doesn't take much to discourage me.

19. **Can you always find the silver lining in every cloud?**

a) No, I don't even look.

b) I suppose so.

c) Yes, of course I can.

20. When you think about it, do you get a good feeling about your life?

a) On the whole I suppose I do.

b) Yes, I love my life.

c) No, frankly I'd rather be having someone else's life.

21. Can you enthuse other members of a team?

a) I might be able to.

b) No problem.

c) I'd be waiting for them to enthuse me.

22. Do people sometimes feel you're a bit of a wet blanket?

a) Never.

b) Not usually. Only if I'm in a bad mood.

c) OK, but you don't have to be so blunt about it.

23. Have people had to bolster your enthusiasm?

a) Yes, all the time.

b) No, it's usually the other way around.

c) Sometimes.

24. Could you communicate enthusiasm even in the face of serious problems?

a) I do it every day.

b) I suppose I could if I tried.

c) No, I'd curl up in a ball.

25. Would you call yourself an enthusiastic person?

a) I couldn't think of a better word.

b) Yes, I hope so.

c) No, and neither would anyone else.

SCORING

	1	2	3		1	2	3		1	2	3
1	b	c	a	10	a	b	c	19	a	b	c
2	a	b	c	11	b	c	a	20	c	a	b
3	b	c	a	12	a	b	c	21	c	a	b
4	b	c	a	13	b	a	c	22	c	b	a
5	a	b	c	14	c	b	a	23	a	c	b
6	b	c	a	15	b	a	c	24	c	b	a
7	a	b	c	16	b	c	a	25	c	b	a
8	c	b	a	17	a	c	b				
9	b	c	a	18	c	b	a				

SCORING

The maximum score is 75.

70–75

Well, as far as enthusiasm goes you have it all. There is plenty there to help spur you on through all the difficulties that face a genius.

60–69

You're doing pretty well when it comes to enthusiasm. However, you do manage to see the darker side of life, if only in your peripheral vision. At least you know how the rest of us feel!

40–59

You don't have huge enthusiasm. Let's hope your other qualities make up for it.

BELOW 40

You really have a problem, don't you?

GROUP DEPENDENCE

Geniuses tend to be rugged individualists. They have to be because, by definition, they see things and understand things denied to the rest of us. So this test is designed to see how you shape up. Are you the sort of person who can go it alone, or do you prefer the support of friends, family and colleagues? Let's find out.

1. Do you like to party?
a) No, I'd rather read a book.
b) Try to stop me!
c) Yes, but not too often.

2. Would you ever consider a trip to the wilderness alone?
a) No, I'd hate the idea.
b) I might, but I'd be worried.
c) Yes, I'd do that and enjoy it.

3. Do you need the support of your family to bolster your confidence?
a) Doesn't everyone?
b) No, I love my family but my confidence is my own.
c) To some extent but I can manage on my own when I have to.

4. Do you worry about what others think of you?
a) Yes, of course.
b) Well, everyone does to some extent.
c) Never give it a thought.

5. Do you go to work partly for the company of others?
a) Yes, I enjoy the social aspects of work.
b) I like the occasional office party.
c) I tend to avoid all that kind of thing.

6. Would you work alone at home?
a) Yes, I'd love to!
b) I might if I had to.
c) No, it would drive me crazy.

7. Do you enjoy your own company?
a) Yes, in fact I prefer it.
b) I don't mind being alone.
c) I get bored on my own.

8. Do you enjoy large public gatherings?
a) I struggle to avoid them.
b) I don't mind them in moderation.
c) I love them.

9. Do you enjoy playing team games?
a) They're my favourite.
b) I don't mind.
c) I'd rather have a tooth pulled!

10. Could you have swapped places with Robinson Crusoe?
a) Yes, that would suit me fine.
b) I'd go crazy.
c) It would be all right for a week or two.

11. If you could choose, which of these would you do:
a) Go out to a big party.
b) Have a really nice evening at home.
c) Have a few friends round for dinner.

12. Do you feel threatened by the presence of other people?
a) No, I love the company.
b) Not really, but I like my privacy as well.
c) Yes, I hate being with people more than I have to.

13. Would people describe you as a loner?
a) Who me? That's a laugh!
b) No, not really.
c) I suppose they would. What's wrong with that?

14. When you make a decision would you feel the need to check it with your colleagues?
a) What for? It's *my* decision.
b) I would always value help from colleagues.
c) I might ask if I thought it necessary.

15. Do you like shopping?
a) Love it! Retail therapy!
b) I'm quite keen as long as it's not too busy.
c) I have to be dragged kicking and screaming.

16. Would you like to live in a city or a small village?
a) I enjoy the peace of village life.
b) I wouldn't mind either. It would depend on the house.
c) I couldn't live in the country. City life is definitely my thing.

17. Do you take notice of opinion polls?
a) Only so that I can ignore them!
b) Yes, I often take them into account.
c) I do sometimes but I'm quite capable of making up my own mind.

18. Do you ever get lonely?
a) No, I like my own company.
b) Yes, quite often.
c) No, I'm never alone long enough.

19. In terms of contact with people, which of these jobs would suit you best:
a) Stand-up comedian.
b) Office worker.
c) Computer programmer.

20. How often do you go out socializing?
a) Several times a week.
b) Several times a month.
c) Seldom.

21. How often do you invite friends round?
a) Several times a month.
b) All the time.
c) What friends?

22. Do you feel threatened or nervous when you are alone?
a) Yes, it makes me feel very edgy.
b) Not at all.
c) A bit.

23. Would you take a job on a space station for a year with only two other astronauts for company?

a) That would be fascinating.

b) No, I couldn't cope with the isolation.

c) I'd consider it but probably would end up not going.

24. A wonderful house is for sale at a bargain price. The catch? It's miles from anywhere. Would you take it?

a) I don't care about the price, I'm not living out in the wilds.

b) I don't care about the price, I'd want to live there anyway.

c) I'd think about it.

25. What is the longest you have been without speaking to another person?

a) Days. Weeks. I really don't remember.

b) A few hours. I still remember how much I hated it.

c) A couple of days. I was glad to find company again.

SCORING

	1	2	3		1	2	3		1	2	3
1	b	c	a	10	b	c	a	19	a	b	c
2	a	b	c	11	a	c	b	20	a	b	c
3	a	c	b	12	a	b	c	21	b	a	c
4	a	b	c	13	a	b	c	22	a	c	b
5	a	b	c	14	b	c	a	23	b	c	a
6	c	b	a	15	a	b	c	24	a	c	b
7	c	b	a	16	c	b	a	25	b	c	a
8	c	b	a	17	b	c	a				
9	a	b	c	18	b	a	c				

SCORING

The maximum score is 75.

70–75

You just don't need other people or value their company and opinions. You may not be popular but why should you care, you don't even know what it means. You have the self-centred approach that genius requires. No one will ever get to disrupt your work unless they come armed.

60–69

You are quite happy alone and don't really need other people much. But you're no hermit and you are not totally indifferent to others. You will find it easy to shut others out when you have to but also know how to relate to people when it suits you.

40–59

You're quite people-dependent. You don't really enjoy your own company that much and you need the love and support of friends, colleagues and relatives. You don't really have the self-sufficiency to be a genius.

BELOW 40

You did this test with six other people at a party.

INSPIRATION

A genius needs to be inspired. All those bright ideas are going to have to come from somewhere. But where? Are you the sort of person who finds inspiration easily, or do you have to cudgel your brain before it will produce each new notion? This is a test to see just how inspired you are.

1. Do you feel that your work is inspired from 'above' (by God or by your muse, for example)?

a) Yes, of course.

b) No, not at all.

c) Maybe. I haven't given it much thought.

2. Do you get new ideas when you dream?

a) Never.

b) Occasionally.

c) Very often.

3. Do you find that valuable notions just pop into your mind at odd times of the day or night?

a) Very often.

b) It happens from time to time.

c) No, that's not how it works for me.

4. If you listen to a moving piece of music, do you find that it sparks off ideas of your own?

a) Not really.

b) Yes, music is a great source of inspiration.

c) It might do.

5. Do you find that the work of other geniuses has an inspirational effect on you?

a) Yes, of course.

b) That has happened to me.

c) No, I don't find that works for me.

6. Do you have to work hard for your ideas?

a) Yes, it's the only way.

b) No, they come easily.

c) Sometimes I'm lucky but more often it takes hard work.

7. Do you look at a blank sheet of paper (or empty computer screen) for hours with nothing happening?

a) No, fortunately not.

b) Like most people I get stuck sometimes.

c) It happens all the time.

8. Are there certain rituals you go through to get yourself into 'thinking mode'?

a) Yes, that helps.

b) Nothing helps me, I just have to plug away until an idea presents itself.

c) I don't need rituals, the ideas just come of their own accord.

9. Do you have to be in the right mood to get a new idea?

a) No, I don't have to be in any special mood.

b) Yes, it helps to be in the right mood.

c) There is no 'right' mood for me. It's just a hard slog.

10.Do you have the equivalent of 'writer's block' when you can't get any ideas at all?

a) Often.

b) Sometimes.

c) Never.

11.Do you have periods when the ideas come so fast that you have to work through the night to keep up with the creative flow?

a) No, unfortunately not.

b) Only very occasionally.

c) Yes, it happens quite frequently.

12.Do you use any technique, eg. meditation or yoga, to keep your creative juices flowing?

a) They don't flow, they ooze. Slowly! Techniques don't help.

b) My juices flow just fine without extra help.

c) Yes, I find some techniques do help.

13.Are you afraid that one day the creative flow will dry up completely?

a) Yes, it could happen.

b) I can't imagine such a thing.

c) It may have happened already.

14.Do you find that sometimes you have to look to other people to provide your inspiration?

a) Sometimes others can help.

b) I never need anyone else's help.

c) To be honest there is not much anyone can do to help.

15.Is there one person, maybe your partner, who inspires you?

a) Yes, that's true.

b) I keep telling you, I don't need help. Read my lips.

c) It's still a struggle.

16.If you were held in solitary confinement, would your inspiration stop?

a) Nothing but nothing stops my inspiration.

b) Yes, of course it would.

c) Who needs solitary confinement? Mine stops just fine by itself.

17.Is your health linked to the amount of inspiration you receive?

a) Yes, though in my case it's lack of inspiration.

b) Yes, I feel that inspiration keeps me going.

c) I'm constantly inspired and feel fantastic!

18.A great sculptor said that his statues already existed and all he did was chip away the excess stone. Do you ever feel similarly about your work?

a) All the time.

b) I keep chipping away and get nowhere.

c) I know what he means, but it doesn't come that easily to me.

19.Could you continue to live if your inspiration dried up?

a) No, that would be the end for me.

b) I'd struggle on somehow.

c) What do you mean 'if'?

20. Is there one moment in your life so far when you felt you'd had a mental breakthrough?

a) Yes.

b) Definitely not.

c) There have been numerous small victories.

21. Do other people look to you for inspiration?

a) They'd look in vain.

b) Yes, I'm quite flattered that sometimes they do.

c) Of course, all the time.

22. Edison said, 'Genius is 1% inspiration and 99% perspiration.' What do you think?

a) Oh yes, that's me.

b) No, Edison was a talentless slogger.

c) I suppose there's some truth in that.

23. Is inspiration central to your life?

a) Unfortunately not.

b) I'd like to think so.

c) Absolutely.

24. Do you find great art or great science inspiring?

a) Yes, though I don't *need* outside help.

b) Yes, definitely.

c) No. I find them interesting but I still have to work hard for my own ideas.

25. Do you seek constantly for one really huge idea?

a) Yes. In vain.

b) Yes, and I'm hopeful of finding it.

c) No. I've already got it.

SCORING

	1	2	3		1	2	3		1	2	3
1	b	c	a	10	a	b	c	19	c	b	a
2	a	b	c	11	a	b	c	20	b	c	a
3	c	b	a	12	a	c	b	21	a	b	c
4	a	c	b	13	c	a	b	22	a	c	b
5	c	b	a	14	c	a	b	23	a	b	c
6	a	c	b	15	c	a	b	24	c	b	a
7	c	b	a	16	c	b	a	25	a	b	c
8	b	a	c	17	a	b	c				
9	c	b	a	18	b	c	a				

SCORING

The maximum score is 75.

70–75

Your inspiration is very strong. You never lack ideas, just the time to get to grips with them all.

60–69

You have a steady flow of inspiration. You realize that the flow is not unlimited but, in the end, you'll always be OK.

40–59

You have to work for your ideas. Nothing comes easily and you are often afraid that inspiration will dry up completely.

BELOW 40

Ideas do not come to you easily, if at all.

OBSESSIVENESS

For most people, being obsessive is not regarded as a very attractive characteristic. It smacks a little of mental problems. People who are obsessive lack a sense of proportion and get carried away by notions that may not do them any good. However, geniuses ARE obsessive. They have to be or they will never achieve the level of attainment they require. Have a go at this test to see just how obsessive you really are.

1. Do you check repeatedly to see whether you locked the car?

a) Yes, always.

b) Sometimes.

c) No, I'm always sure I locked it.

2. Do you go over your work ceaselessly to try to find mistakes?

a) No, I do a quick check then let it go.

b) Yes, that's me, I can never check enough.

c) I check things over a few times but eventually you have to let it go.

3. Would you hesitate forever before letting someone else examine your work?

a) No, it's not a problem for me.

b) Yes, I hate that point where you have to let someone else look at your work.

c) I know what you mean, but it's not a major problem.

4. Do you sometimes have notions that you just cannot let go of?

a) No, that doesn't happen to me.

b) It has happened but not a lot.

c) Yes, I feel like that a lot.

5. Do you have ideas that seem more important to you than anything else?

a) Of course, doesn't everyone?

b) No, that's not a problem I have.

c) Some of my ideas seem pretty important but I may be wrong.

6. Do you sometimes get so involved in what you're doing that you forget to eat?

a) No, that's never happened.

b) Very occasionally.

c) I miss meals all the time like that.

7. Have you ever worked so hard on something that you discover you stayed up all night without meaning to?

a) Yes, I frequently forget to go to bed.

b) No, I'm always ready for bed at the same time.

c) It has happened from time to time.

8. Are there certain things which you just have to do, although there is no logical reason for your actions?

a) Yes, it can be embarrassing but I can't stop it.

b) No, I don't do that.

c) I have had that experience but not often.

158

9. Do you get stuck with one thought to the exclusion of all else?

a) Not really.

b) From time to time.

c) Yes, that's just the way I am.

10. Are you sometimes unaware of what goes on around you because you are so involved in what you are doing?

a) Yes, that's me all over.

b) No, that's not the way I am.

c) It happens occasionally.

11. Will you follow a train of thought even though others try to convince you it is misguided?

a) Yes, once I start nothing's going to stop me.

b) I'm like that sometimes.

c) No, that really isn't me.

12. Have people told you that you tend to become obsessive about things?

a) No, I don't get told that.

b) It has been mentioned.

c) Yes, that's said about me all the time.

13. Are there issues that you just cannot leave alone even though pursuing them is of no obvious benefit to you?

a) No, I would know when to stop.

b) I recognize that situation.

c) That's me all the time.

14. Does one issue dominate your whole life?

a) Of course.

b) Not at all.

c) Yes, though I can switch off when I need to.

15. Do you find it hard to switch off from things you think are important?

a) Yes, switching off isn't in my nature.

b) It's usually possible for me to switch off.

c) No, I that isn't a problem.

16. Do you find yourself checking and re-checking the details of what you have done?

a) I do that compulsively.

b) I sometimes do it but can usually stop myself.

c) No I'm never tempted to do that.

17. On a scale of 1 – 10, how obsessive do you think you are? (1 = really laid back, 10 = totally obsessive)

a) 1 – 3.

b) 4 – 7.

c) 8 – 10.

18. Does your tendency to get stuck with one thought irritate people?

a) Yes, hugely.

b) No, I don't think so.

c) Sometimes.

19. Have you ever had medical treatment for obsessive/compulsive disorders?

a) Yes.

b) No.

c) It was a long time ago.

20. Have your obsessions ever had a detrimental effect on your life?

a) No, certainly not.

b) Yes, unfortunately.

c) Once or twice.

21.Have you ever wished that you could be less caught up in the issues which concern you?

a) Yes, often.

b) No, never.

c) Sometimes.

22.Do you ever feel satisfied that you have done enough work on a project?

a) No, not at all.

b) Yes, eventually.

c) Of course.

23.Do you find it quite impossible just to let go?

a) Yes.

b) No.

c) Sometimes.

24.Have people broken off relationships with you because of your obsessive behaviour?

a) Yes, I'm afraid that has happened to me repeatedly.

b) No, I've never had that misfortune.

c) Yes, it has happened, but not often.

25.Do you regard your single-mindedness as a great asset?

a) Yes, I find it invaluable.

b) No, that isn't one of my virtues.

c) It's quite useful, but I'm not that single-minded.

SCORING

	1	2	3		1	2	3		1	2	3
1	c	b	a	10	b	c	a	19	b	c	a
2	a	c	b	11	c	b	a	20	a	c	b
3	a	c	b	12	a	b	c	21	b	c	a
4	a	b	c	13	a	b	c	22	c	b	a
5	b	c	a	14	b	c	a	23	b	c	a
6	a	b	c	15	c	b	a	24	b	c	a
7	b	c	a	16	c	b	a	25	b	c	a
8	b	c	a	17	a	b	c				
9	a	b	c	18	b	c	a				

SCORING

The maximum score is 75.

70–75

You have the obsessive quality needed to become a genius, but beware of sliding into mental illness because of your obsessions.

60–69

You're very obsessive but not entirely blind to other issues. You are aware that there may be dangers in being so single-minded.

40–59

You are quite obsessive on certain subjects but are well aware that there are many other things that should occupy your mind.

BELOW 40

Forget it! You have the mental tension of a shrimping net.

SELF-IMAGE

When considering your genius potential, it would be a good idea to think about your self-image for a while. The following test is designed to help you with that task. The questions are designed to help you crystallize what you feel about yourself and, in particular, whether you feel as if you have the potential to be a genius.

1. Do you feel that you have been in some way 'chosen'?

a) Yes, I've always known that there is something special about me.

b) No, not at all.

c) I've sometimes had a sneaking suspicion that there is more to me than people suspect.

2. Do you excel in any activity at all?

a) No, not really.

b) Yes, I have abilities well above the average.

c) I'm not sure. I might not have found the right activity yet.

3. Does fame attract you?

a) I've never given it much thought.

b) I'd just love to be famous.

c) I'd absolutely hate it.

4. Have people ever picked you out as special?

a) Yes, sometimes I've been noticed.

b) No, not really.

c) Yes, people have often mentioned my abilities.

5. Do you have one interest that completely dominates your life?

a) Yes, there's one subject about which I'm completely passionate.

b) No, I tend to be interested in lots of things.

c) I have a few quite serious interests.

6. Do you sometimes feel that you know better than other people?

a) Never. I'd hate to feel like that.

b) Yes, sometimes I get impatient when I feel I know more.

c) It's awful to admit it, but I feel that way almost all the time.

7. Do ideas interest you just for their own sake?

a) No, I'm not really an ideas person.

b) I like ideas but I'm also quite practical.

c) Ideas just fascinate me.

8. Are you good at abstract thought?

a) Yes, I've always been able to think in the abstract.

b) No, I'm far too practical in my outlook.

c) I'm not bad but not outstanding.

9. Do you secretly suspect you may be a genius?

a) Yes, but I keep quiet about it.

b) No, not at all.

c) Just sometimes I think I might be.

10. Would it worry you that no one might discover your talents until after you were dead?

a) Yes, I hate that idea.
b) Never thought about it.
c) It doesn't bother me too much.

11. Would the idea of posthumous fame attract you?

a) No, not at all. What good would it do me?
b) I suppose it would be quite nice to be remembered.
c) Yes, I'd love it if I thought people would remember me.

12. Would you rather have a good night out or stay home and study?

a) I'd give up most things for the sake of studying.
b) I'd take the night out.
c) I might stay in if it was important.

13. Do you think you have an original mind?

a) Not really.
b) Yes, I really believe I do.
c) I'm not too sure about this.

14. Do people find your ideas interesting?

a) No, they don't.
b) Some people have said so.
c) Yes, people are always keen to hear what I have to say.

15. Do you sometimes feel people cannot grasp what you're saying?

a) Yes, it bothers me a lot.
b) No, I don't have that problem.
c) Yes, it happens sometimes.

16. Are you frustrated with your life and feel capable of doing more?

a) No, I'm really quite happy with things as they are.
b) I'd sometimes like to do more.
c) Yes, I long to reach my full potential.

17. Do you generally feel good about yourself?

a) Yes, all the time.
b) No, not that often.
c) Mostly.

18. Do you feel you have a valuable contribution to make to the future of the world?

a) Yes, I'm sure of it.
b) No, I doubt it very much.
c) I hope so, but I'm not sure.

19. Are you good at overcoming adversity?

a) No, not really.
b) Yes, I fight through anything.
c) I try really hard when things are difficult.

20. Do you believe strongly in your own ability?

a) Yes, I never doubt myself.
b) I usually believe in myself.
c) No, I tend to be rather self-doubting.

21. Do you constantly struggle to develop yourself?

a) Yes, all the time.
b) I think about it quite a lot.
c) No, I'm not that bothered.

22. Are you thirsty for new knowledge?

a) No, I don't do much about new learning.

b) Yes, I'm passionate about discovering new things.

c) I'm quite interested in developing my knowledge.

23. Do you keep up with the latest developments in your field?

a) Of course, always.

b) No, I don't have time.

c) I try to but don't always succeed.

24. Do people come to you for advice in areas where you have special abilities?

a) Yes, frequently.

b) No, that never happens to me.

c) It does happen from time to time.

25. Do you know how intelligent you are?

a) Yes, I had my IQ tested and it's very high.

b) Yes, I think I'm pretty bright.

c) No, never bothered to find out.

SCORING

	1	2	3		1	2	3		1	2	3		1	2	3
1	b	c	a	8	b	c	a	15	b	c	a	22	a	c	b
2	a	c	b	9	b	c	a	16	a	b	c	23	b	c	a
3	c	a	b	10	b	c	a	17	b	c	a	24	b	c	a
4	b	a	c	11	a	b	c	18	b	c	a	25	c	b	a
5	b	c	a	12	b	c	a	19	a	c	b				
6	a	b	c	13	a	c	b	20	c	b	a				
7	a	b	c	14	a	b	c	21	c	b	a				

SCORING

The maximum score is 75.

70–75

You feel good about yourself and have a pretty shrewd idea of your own worth.

60–69

You do not suffer many doubts but you are smart enough to know that you don't get it right all the time.

40–59

You don't really have the level of self-belief to be a genius.

BELOW 40

You don't have much opinion of yourself. Put your feet up and relax – a genius you're not.

VISION

To be a genius you have to have vision. Do you? Can you see the big picture? Do you see possibilities that others miss? Can you understand issues more deeply than other people? Try this test and find out if you have the vision to be a genius.

1. Do you often understand things that other people miss?

a) Yes, that happens to me all the time.

b) I've had that experience from time to time.

c) No, I can't say that happens to me.

2. Can you see subtleties in situations others overlook?

a) No, not really.

b) Yes, that's me.

c) It happens sometimes.

3. Do you have thoughts others simply cannot understand?

a) No, never.

b) All the time.

c) Occasionally.

4. Would you regard yourself as being ahead of your time?

a) Not really.

b) To some extent.

c) Without doubt.

5. Do you get impatient because people cannot follow your reasoning?

a) No, that doesn't happen to me.

b) It happens, though not often.

c) Yes, that's what I'm like.

6. Would you regard yourself as a visionary thinker?

a) Yes, definitely.

b) No, I can't say I am.

c) I have my moments.

7. Do bright ideas flood into your mind all the time?

a) Constantly.

b) Seldom.

c) Sometimes.

8. Do you often find yourself developing new concepts?

a) No, not really.

b) Yes, always.

c) Quite often.

9. Do other people feel that you have something new and unusual to say?

a) Yes, I think they do.

b) No, I doubt it.

c) It has been known.

10. Are you widely recognized as an innovator?

a) No, I couldn't claim that.

b) Yes, of course.

c) Maybe sometimes.

11. Have your ideas been published in any form?

a) Yes, frequently.

b) Yes, once or twice.

c) No, never.

12. Do you get frustrated by being so far ahead of popular thinking that people misunderstand you?

a) That hasn't happened to me.

b) Yes, it drives me crazy.

c) I have certainly had that problem sometimes.

13. Are your ideas known in countries other than your own?

a) Not at all.

b) Yes, I have an international reputation.

c) I am known overseas but only to a select few.

14. Have you developed concepts of global significance?

a) One or two.

b) None.

c) Yes, of course my work is of world importance.

15. Would you feel confident enough in your ideas to lecture to an audience of top experts in your field?

a) I have done frequently.

b) No, I'd rather not.

c) I might pluck up the courage.

16. Could you explain your ideas in simple language that anyone could understand?

a) Yes, I suppose so.

b) My ideas are extremely complex and not really for the lay person.

c) I might be able to explain, but it would be hard.

17. Do you expect people to have heard of you in 100 years' time?

a) Not, I don't think so.

b) They might have done.

c) Yes, unless they're living in a monastery.

18. Will your ideas revolutionize the way we live?

a) I should hope so.

b) I doubt it.

c) I would be amazed if they didn't.

19. Do you get laughed at because people are just unable to understand your thought processes?

a) Yes, but who cares?

b) It's a problem sometimes.

c) No, not really.

20. Do you think that you have thoughts which will change the world for the better?

a) I hope so.

b) Not sure.

c) I have no doubt of it whatever.

21. Can you formulate concepts that will revolutionise modern science, mathematics or philosophy?

a) Of course.

b) I might.

c) No, I don't think so.

22. Are you an artist whose vision will change the way people think about art?

a) Yes, that's my mission in life.
b) No, that's not me.
c) I hope that happens, but I'm not sure.

23. Do you feel that you have within you the seeds of genius?

a) I doubt it.
b) I think that maybe I do.
c) I tell myself so every day.

24. Will your ideas be recognized within your lifetime?

a) Probably not.
b) Possibly.
c) They'd better be!

25. Do you get the recognition you deserve?

a) Not entirely.
b) Yes, I think so.
c) Yes, but I will get even more in future.

SCORING

	1	2	3		1	2	3		1	2	3		1	2	3
1	c	b	a	8	a	c	b	15	b	c	a	22	b	c	a
2	a	c	b	9	b	c	a	16	a	c	b	23	a	b	c
3	a	c	b	10	a	c	b	17	a	b	c	24	a	b	c
4	a	b	c	11	c	b	a	18	b	a	c	25	a	b	c
5	a	b	c	12	a	c	b	19	c	b	a				
6	b	c	a	13	a	c	b	20	b	a	c				
7	b	c	a	14	b	a	c	21	c	b	a				

SCORING

The maximum score is 75.

70–75

Yes! You are truly a visionary thinker. You have complete faith in your vision and that is what matters for a genius.

60–69

You are pretty sure of your status as a visionary but are not immune to self-doubt.

40–59

You aren't really enough of a visionary for genius. You have good ideas but, at the end of the day, you know you are not major league.

BELOW 40

Don't give up the day job.

GENIUS GYM

This is the section of the book where you can put all those grey cells to work. What we have here is not just a selection of puzzles. After all, what self-respecting genius would waste time on those? No, this section contains some brain-bustingly difficult problems which will tax your mental powers to the limit. The idea is not just to give you the fun of solving them (and you will have fun), but also to give you some valuable insights into unusual mind sets and ways of tackling problems.

What is notable about these puzzles is the way in which they are all constructed from quite simple elements - usually a few digits or letters. What is notable is that with such trivial bits and pieces it is possible to produce puzzles of great complexity which can keep very intelligent people completely baffled for hours. OK, now it's time to see how well you cope with our mental training course. Good luck!

Letter labyrinth

These little word puzzles show just how difficult an apparently simple problem may become when you are deprived of some information. In each case the problem is the same, you must take a letter from each cloud in turn and make a word.

Puzzle 1

There are five 5-letter words to be made. It will help your search considerably when you're told that they all have something to do with the arts.

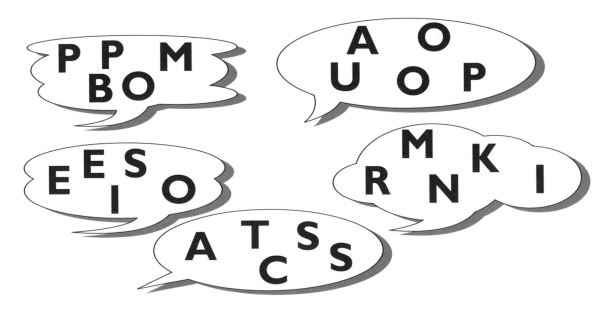

Puzzle 2

Now see the difference. Here are another 5 five-letter words but this time there is no theme to help you.

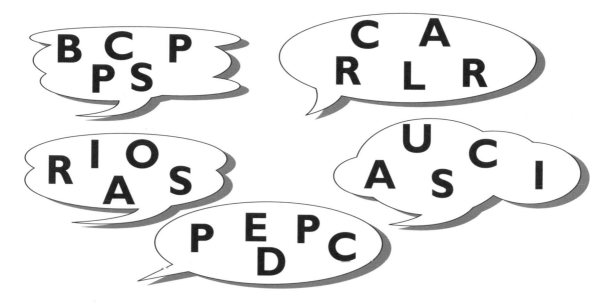

Puzzle 3

Now try some 6-letter words. Again there is no common theme to help you.

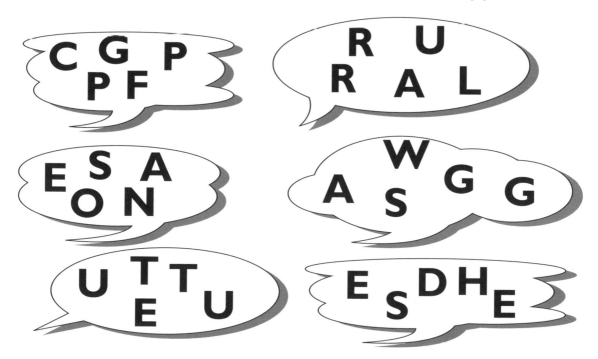

Puzzle 4

Now for a real test. There are some 6-letter words but among them we have distributed a set of nonsense letters. Can you sort that lot out?

Triangle terror

The humble triangle puzzle is a classic and a delight. It was first designed by that genius Harold Gale (late and much loved CEO of British Mensa) many years ago and is still going strong. Its main virtue is that it looks simple, yet it may range in difficulty from childishly easy to fiendishly difficult - and you can't tell just by looking which is which! Its other feature is that it can change tack without warning (as you are about to find out). The basic puzzle is just a simple calculation like, 'Take A from B, multiply by C and put the result in the middle of the triangle'. Easy? It's surprising just how long it can take to work out even one of these simple triangles. Then it gets harder. There are, as you might suppose, countless variations as to what you can do with the numbers and where you might put the results of your calculations. You don't have to treat the triangles as separate, you can interlink them so that, for example, the result of one calculation goes in the next triangle to its right. Just when the solver is feeling confident about all this the numbers change to letters. What could that mean? Well, they could represent numbers (based on their position in the alphabet, for example), on the other hand you might find that the whole game has changed beyond recognition.

The reason that such puzzles are so useful in genius training is that they teach you to stay mentally alert. Never overlook what is staring you in the face. Be aware of subtleties but don't end up being too clever for your own good. Tough isn't it? But then what fun would it be if just anyone could do it?

Puzzle 5

This, I promise, is just a simple one to get you started. A few seconds work should solve it.

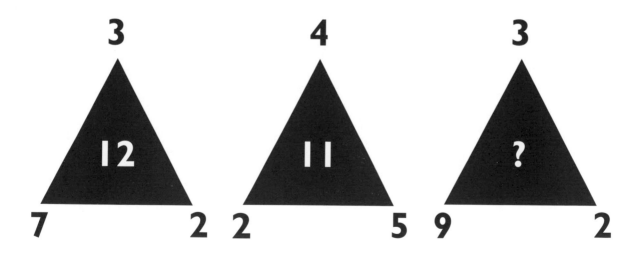

Puzzle 6

This one is just that little bit more difficult. The principle is the same but the formula will take you longer to find.

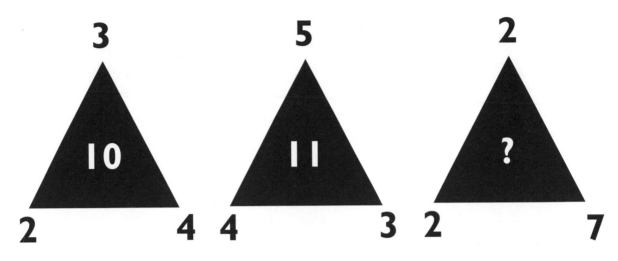

Puzzle 7

Now we come to a new variation. The formula is perfectly simple but then we did something sneaky to the answer.

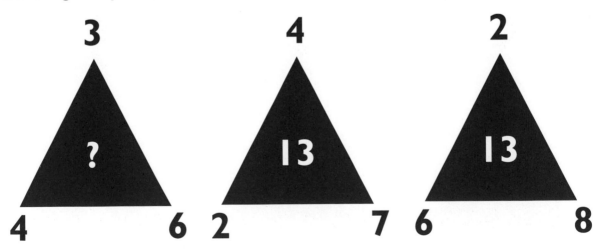

Puzzle 8

Now what? The formula is still very simple but you need ingenuity to work out what we've done to complicate matters.

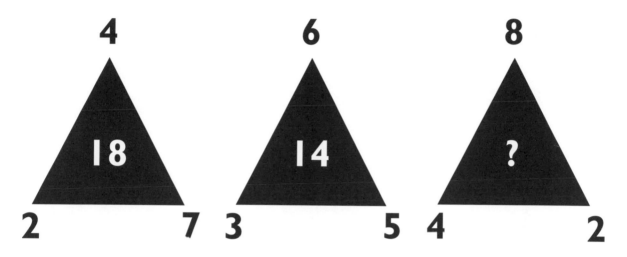

Puzzle 9

Now the numbers change to letters. Does that bother you? No, not really. But be careful.

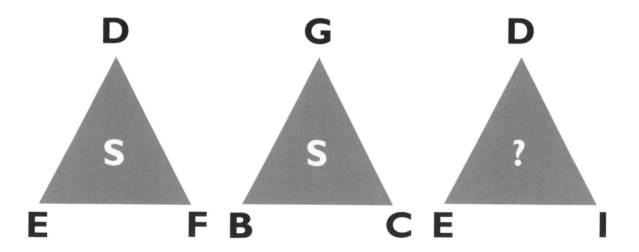

172

Puzzle 10
Got the hang of it now have you? Try another.

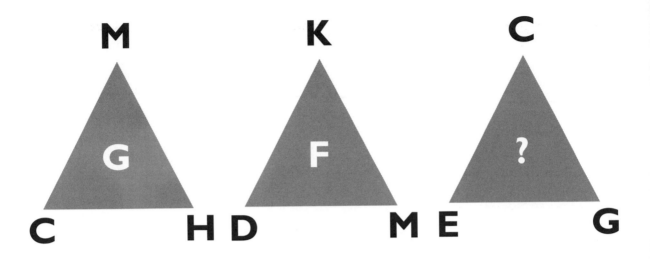

Puzzle 11
What the heck's gone wrong here? Just when you thought you'd got the whole thing sussed!

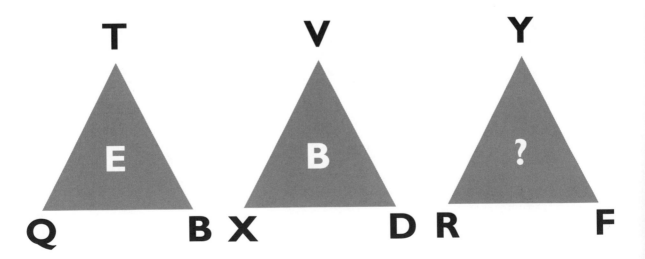

Puzzle 12

OK, you may have guessed what we've done to the letters, but the formula is interesting.

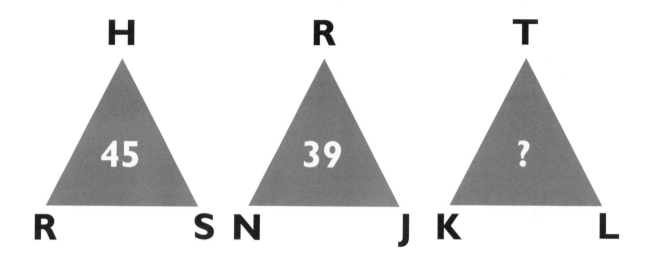

Puzzle 13

What now? This is the point at which you need to take stock of the situation. Don't let your mind run along those same old rails!

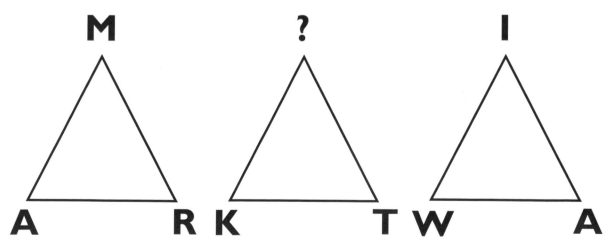

Puzzle 14

Even when people know how this one works, they can overlook the obvious.

Circles

Like the triangles puzzle, the circles below are capable of great variation and increasing complexity. The lesson is the same: never take anything for granted. Only by keeping an open mind will you be able to unravel the complexities of these problems.

Puzzle 15

This is just a simple calculation. There is a very small 'twist' to it but, even so, it should take you a couple of seconds to work out what is going on.

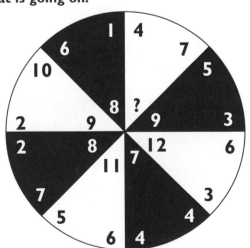

Puzzle 16

Another quite simple variation. A few seconds should be enough to work this out.

Puzzle 17

This is still the same idea but here is yet another variation.

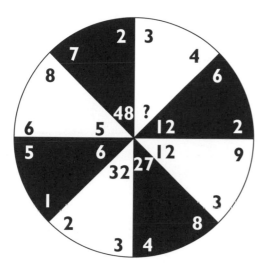

Puzzle 18

Now it's starting to get rather more difficult. The calculation needed is trivial but the logic involved in cracking the puzzle takes some thinking out.

Puzzle 19

OK, now we're playing hard ball. Once again the calculation could be done by a five-year-old but the logic needed is now really taxing.

Puzzle 20

Yet another fiendish variation. Before you bend your brain to solving this one, pause for a moment to admire the sheer versatility of this apparently harmless little puzzle.

Matrix mayhem

The first section is a set of matrices. A matrix is just a grid containing information. In this case we have filled each grid in with a sequence of numbers or letters but have left some of the squares blank. Your job is to work out the logic that was used in compiling the matrix and replace the blanks. Easy? Initially, yes. Then it's gets harder, and harder, and very much harder.

Puzzle 21

A	C	D	B	A	C	D	B	A	C	D	B	A	C	D
B	A	C	D	B	A	C	D	B	A	C	D	B	A	C
D	B	A	C	D	B	A	C	D	B	A	C	D	B	A
C	D	B	A	C	D	B	A	C	D	B	A	C	D	B
A	C	D	B	A	C	D	B	A	C	D	B	A	C	D
B	A	C	D	B	A			A	C	D	B	A	C	
D	B	A	C	D	B			B	A	C	D	B	A	
C	D	B	A	C	D			D	B	A	C	D	B	
A	C	D	B	A	C	D	B	A	C	D	B	A	C	D
B	A	C	D	B	A	C	D	B	A	C	D	B	A	C
D	B	A	C	D	B	A	C	D	B	A	C	D	B	A
C	D	B	A	C	B	B	A	C	D	B	A	C	D	B
A	C	D	B	A	C	D	B	A	C	D	B	A	C	D
B	A	C	D	B	A	C	D	B	A	C	D	B	A	C
D	B	A	C	D	B	A	C	D	B	A	C	D	B	A

Puzzle 22

1	4	3	2	1	4	3	2	1	4	3	2	1	4	3
4	1	2	3	4	1	2	3	4	1	2				2
3	2	1	4	3	2	1	4	3	2	1				1
2	3	4	1	2	3	4	1	2	3	4				4
1	4	3	2	1	4	3	2	1	4	3	2	1	4	3
4	1	2	3	4	1	2	3	4	1	2	3	4	1	2
3	2	1	4	3	2	1	4	3	2	1	4	3	2	1
2	3	4	1	2	3	4	1	2	3	4	1	2	3	4
1	4	3	2	1	4	3	2	1	4	3	2	1	4	3
4	1	2	3	4	1	2	3	4	1	2	3	4	1	2
3	2	1	4	3	2	1	4	3	2	1	4	3	2	1
2	3	4	1	2	3	4	1	2	3	4	1	2	3	4
1	4	3	2	1	4	3	2	1	4	3	2	1	4	3
4	1	2	3	4	1	2	3	4	1	2	3	4	1	2
3	2	1	4	3	2	1	4	3	2	1	4	3	2	1

Puzzle 23

F	X	F	X	P	F	A	L	P	F	F	X	F	X	P
A	P	A	L	X	X	P	L	X	P	A	P	A	L	F
L	L	A	A	F	F	A	A	L	L	L	L	A	X	X
P	X	L	P	X	X	L	A	P	A	P	X	A	F	A
F	P	L	A	F	P	X	F	X	F	F	L	P	L	P
F	A	L				X	F	X	P	P	L	P	L	F
X	P	L				P	A	L	F	A	F	A	X	L
F	A	A				L	A	X	X	X	X	A	A	P
X	L	A	P	A	P	X	A	F	A	F	L	X	F	L
P	X	F	X	F	F	L	P	L	P	P	F	X	A	P
F	X	F	X	P	P	L	P	L	F	P	A	X	F	P
A	P	A	L	F	A	F	A	X	L	L	F	X	L	F
L	L	A	X	X	X	X	A	A	P	P	A	A	X	X
P	X	A	F	A	F	L	X	F	L	L	X	A	F	A
F	L	P	L	P	P	F	X	A	P	F	L	P	L	P

Puzzle 24

Z	T	A	B	X	Z	T	A	B	X	Z	T	A	B	X
Z	T	A	B	X	Z	T	A	B	X	Z	T	A	B	Z
X	B	X	Z	T	A	B	X	Z	T	A	B	X	X	T
B	A	B	X	Z	T	A	B	X	Z	T	A	Z	Z	A
A	T	A	Z	T	A	B	X	Z	T	A	B	T	T	B
T	Z	T	X	X	Z	T	A				X	A	A	X
Z	X	Z	B	B	Z	T	A				Z	B	B	Z
X	B	X	A	A	X	B	X				T	X	X	T
B	A	B	T	T	B	A	T	Z	A	T	A	Z	Z	A
A	T	A	Z	Z	A	T	Z	X	B	A	B	T	T	B
T	Z	T	X	X	B	A	T	Z	X	B	X	A	A	X
Z	X	Z	B	A	T	Z	X	B	A	T	Z	B	B	Z
X	B	X	B	A	T	Z	X	B	A	T	Z	X	X	T
B	A	T	Z	X	B	A	T	Z	X	B	A	T	Z	A
A	T	Z	X	B	A	T	Z	X	B	A	T	Z	X	B

Puzzle 25

V	A	U	V	V	P	C	T	T	U	A	B	B	C	P
B	T	P	U	V	B	U	C	V	V	C	A	T	V	V
C	V	T	A	A	V	B	P	P	T	V	U	U	A	B
A	C	B	V	P	A	V	V	U	P	V	T	B	A	C
B	C	P	V	V	A	U	V	V	P	C	C	V	T	A
T	V	A	P	B	T	P	U	V	B	T	P	U	V	B
U	B	V	C	C	V	T	A	A	U	V	V	P	C	T
C	U	T	B	A	C	B	V	V	U	P	V	T	C	U
T	U	A	B	B	C	P	P	T	V	U	U	B	V	C
V	V	C	A	T	V	V	C	A	T	V	A	P	B	T
P	T	V	U	U	A	B	B			V	A	U	V	
U	P	V	T	B	A	C	B			V	V	U	P	
V	P	C	C	V	T	A	A			P	T	V	U	
V	B	T	P	U	V	B	U	C	V	V	C	A	T	V
A	U	V	V	P	C	T	T	U	A	B	B	C	P	V

Puzzle 26

3	9	5	6	4	2	3	9	5	6	4	2	3	9	5
2	4	2	3	9	5	6	4	2	3	9	5	6	4	6
4	6	4	2	3	9	5	6	4	2	3	9	5	2	4
6	5	6	3	9	5	6	4	2	3	9	5	6	3	2
5	9				2	3	9	5	6	4	6	4	9	3
9	3				4	2	3	9	5	2	4	2	5	9
3	2				6	3	9	5	6	3	2	3	6	5
2	4	2	5	9	5	2	4	6	4	9	3	9	4	6
4	6	4	9	3	9	3	2	4	2	5	9	5	2	4
6	5	6	3	2	4	6	5	9	3	6	5	6	3	2
5	9	5	2	4	6	5	9	3	2	4	6	4	9	3
9	3	9	3	2	4	6	5	9	3	2	4	2	5	9
3	2	4	6	5	9	3	2	4	6	5	9	3	6	5
2	4	6	5	9	3	2	4	6	5	9	3	2	4	6
3	2	4	6	5	9	3	2	4	6	5	9	3	2	4

Lateral thinking

The psychologist and author Edward DeBono coined the term 'lateral thinking' back in the '70s. It described a sort of twist of logic which helped the thinker to reach a conclusion that was unavailable to the plodding, step-by-step logic that we so often use. For a while lateral thinking problems became a favourite party game amongst students and young professionals. If you're old enough to have read 'Gravity's Rainbow' or worn flared jeans (the last time they were fashionable), then you probably played this game. If so, then treat yourself to a wander down memory lane and see if your wits are as sharp as they used to be. If this is all new to you - enjoy!

Puzzle 27

Two brothers got off opposite ends of a train and made their way to the booking hall where they met their father. All three greeted each other warmly, climbed into a car, and went home. The odd thing is that, until they met at the station, they had never seen one another before. Who were the men? How had they recognized each other at the station? What can you deduce about their family relationships?

Puzzle 28

Sophie had kittens. Her young owner, Mark, was delighted. However, as the kittens grew, they never played with balls of wool, hunted each other round the garden, or did any of the other playful and amusing things associated with young cats. Mark was quite disappointed but, being only three, he did not quite understand what was wrong with his kittens. What was the problem?

Puzzle 29

Grandpa Joe lay seriously ill in hospital with his relatives gathered around his bed. At exactly 12.13am the clock on the bedside table stopped and grandpa died. Why?

Puzzle 30

Charlie's teacher was taken ill before the last lesson and the class was let out early. She came home before her parents got back from work. As she didn't have a key to get into the house, she played ball in the garden. Unfortunately she threw one ball right through the living room window. However, when her parents came back later there was no sign of the ball. As Charlie could not possibly have entered the house without cutting herself on the jagged glass, her parents believed that she could not have broken the window. Where had the ball gone?

Puzzle 31

A car sped down a steep hill and smashed into a brick wall at the bottom at over 80mph. By the time the police arrived, the driver was calmly getting out of what remained of the car clutching his briefcase. Apart from a few cuts and bruises he was unhurt. 'I've seen a few accidents in my time,' said Sergeant O'Reilly 'and by rights you should be dead.' Why did he get away so lightly?

Puzzle 32

A tourist from Spain suffered pains in his stomach. The doctor had been born in Goa but had settled in England years ago. When the tourist went back to his hotel, what was the landlady, who was from Israel, watching on TV?

Puzzle 33

Sam had been staying with his friend Joe for a few days. One day, while Joe was out, the phone rang. When Sam picked it up he heard someone say, 'You must come to 27 Holland Park Lane urgently. And bring the beer, we need it.' With that the caller rang off. Sam searched around and, sure enough, he found a few crates of beer in the garage. He loaded them into his car and drove to the address he'd heard on the phone. But when he got there he found he'd made a dreadful mistake. What was it?

Puzzle 34

A teacher decided to set his pupils an unusual problem. He presented them with a wooden box (with a lid) and the following question: 'There's something I could put in this box that would make it lighter. In fact, the more of these things I put in, the lighter it would become. Also, however many of these things I put in the box, it would remain empty. What things are they?'

Puzzle 35

Becky and her family were very religious. In fact they never missed a chance of going to worship. One Sunday there was a terrible accident. A light aircraft crashed into the very building where Becky's family always attended morning service. The pilot died and there were many injured. Becky's aunt saw the story on the local news and immediately phoned Becky's mum to say, 'You had a lucky escape there, didn't you?' How did she know that the family were not among the injured? They were not mentioned in the TV report and they had not been in contact with anyone else since the accident.

Puzzle 36

An Italian Jewish family emigrated to Israel and set up a restaurant. They thought of a witty and original name which combined their national food with their ethnic background. What did they call it? Clue: the answer is a Yiddish word which most people know irrespective of their ethnic origins.

Pyramids

Another very adaptable puzzle is the pyramid. In fact it is just a collection of triangles which permits the puzzle setter to introduce some interesting complications to the formulae needed to find the solutions. Once again, all the calculations needed are childishly simple, but the real test comes in working out the sequences in which the triangles are used.

Puzzle 37

The first puzzle is quite simple. It involves finding the logic of a simple series and then unravelling the sequence in which the triangles have been filled in.

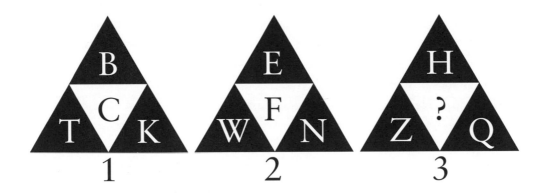

Puzzle 38

This time the series is rather more challenging.

Puzzle 39

The series is quite simple but the use of triangles now becomes more of a challenge.

Puzzle 40

You should have the hang of this by now.

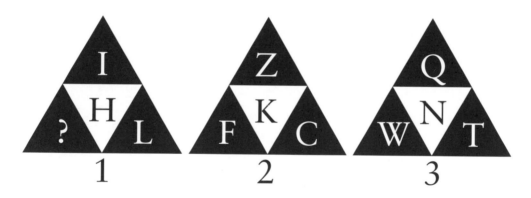

Puzzle 41

This is another just the same.

Puzzle 42

OK, you think you have these figured now? Try this one.

Puzzle 43

Now think about this one. Notice anything strange?

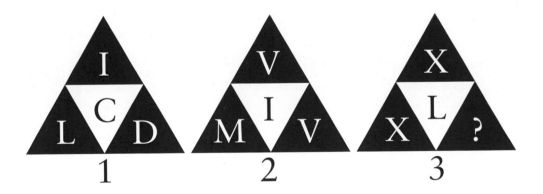

Squares

As we have seen elsewhere, it is quite possible to construct really challenging puzzles with nothing more than a few triangles. Just think what can be achieved with squares! With one more figure to bring into the equation and one more corner to add to the solving sequence, the possibilities are almost endless. Try some and see how you get on. To understand the solutions you should imagine that each square is labelled A, B, C, D, working clockwise from the top left corner.

Puzzle 44

Puzzle 45

Puzzle 46

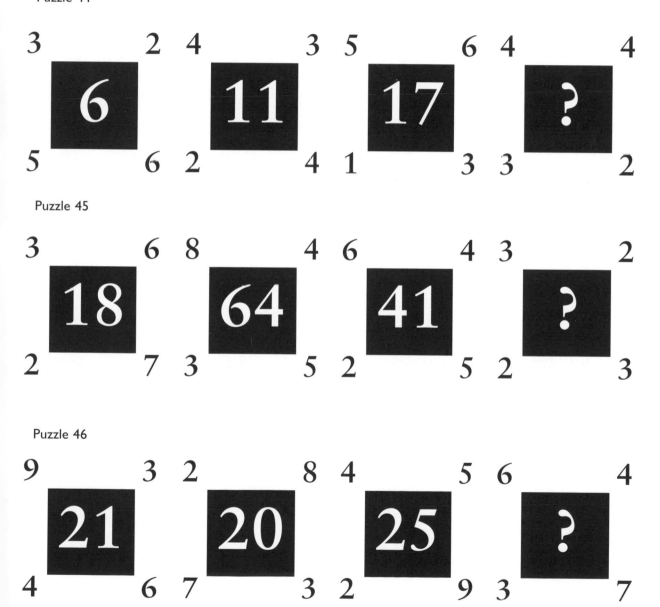

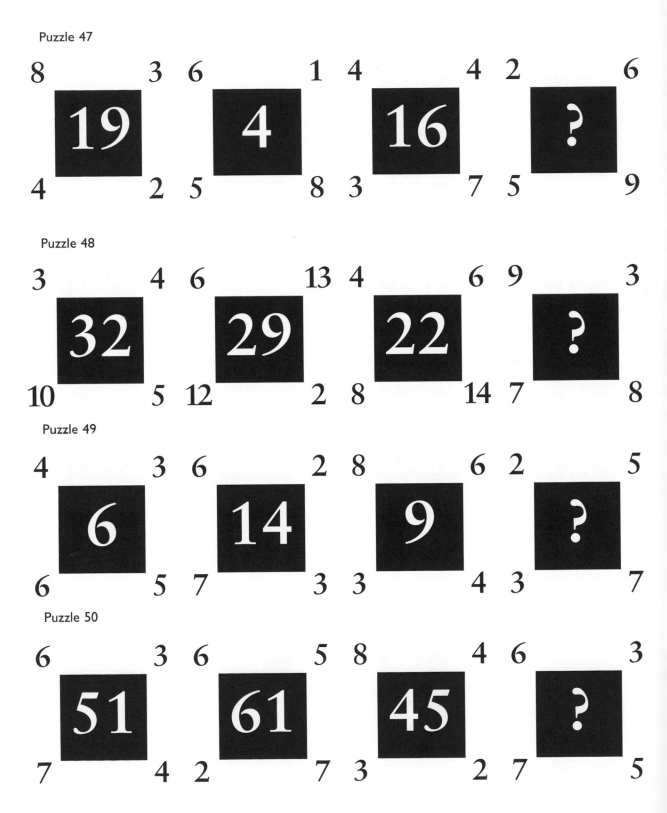

Puzzle 47

8 19 3	6 4 1	4 16 4	2 ? 6
4 2	5 8	3 7	5 9

Puzzle 48

3 32 4	6 29 13	4 22 6	9 ? 3
10 5	12 2	8 14	7 8

Puzzle 49

4 6 3	6 14 2	8 9 6	2 ? 5
6 5	7 3	3 4	3 7

Puzzle 50

6 51 3	6 61 5	8 45 4	6 ? 3
7 4	2 7	3 2	7 5

Puzzle 51

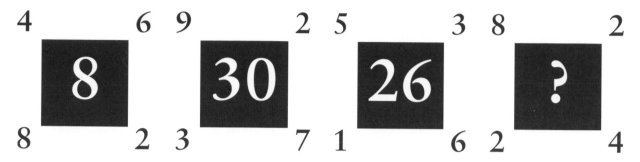

Grids

These grids work in a variety of ways. The first couple are spatial puzzles. Then we have some which depend upon finding links between letters. Finally there are a number in which words have been hidden in the grids.

Puzzle 52

This is a simple spatial puzzle. Discover the sequence in which the dot moves.

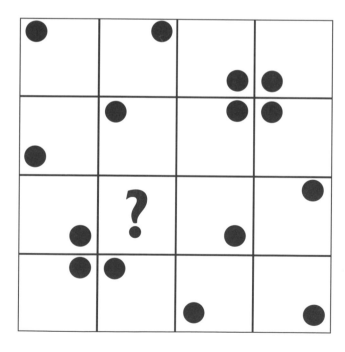

Puzzle 53

Here is a slightly more challenging example.

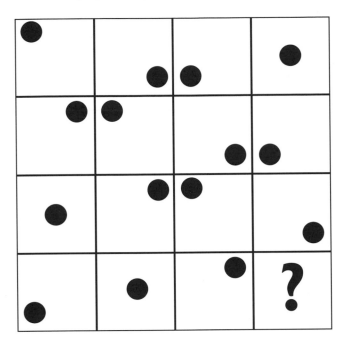

Puzzle 54

This one is even more difficult but, yet again, it is a matter of working out the sequence of moves.

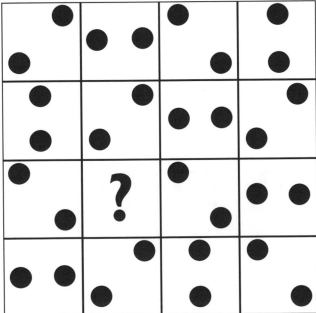

Puzzle 55

Look at the letters carefully and try to work out what they represent.

J	F	M	A
D	S	A	M
N	S	W	J
O	S	A	J

Puzzle 56

Once again take a good look at the letters in the grid and try to work out what they stand for.

O	S	M	M
V	J	S	E
P	O	U	N
N	N	V	U

All these grids have words hidden in them. What makes it difficult is that you do not know how many letters each word has, but you are required to find words to fit broad topics. However, each grid contains three complete words with no letters left over, apart from Puzzles 58, 61 and 67 which have two words, and Puzzle 68, which has just one. Be warned – some of the words used are quite uncommon.

Puzzle 57
topics:
music,
music,
music

S	V	E	Z
A	T	H	Y
R	E	M	S
A	E	N	R

Puzzle 58
topics:
chemistry,
music

C	K	S	P
M	E	O	L
E	R	I	N
A	L	O	A

Puzzle 59
topics:
craft,
human quality,
religion

B	R	U	J
E	E	A	G
L	E	E	N
Z	J	C	E

Puzzle 60
topics:
game,
timespan,
creature

P	U	S	U
U	T	I	L
Q	N	M	T
U	R	G	E

Puzzle 61
topics:
chemistry,
business

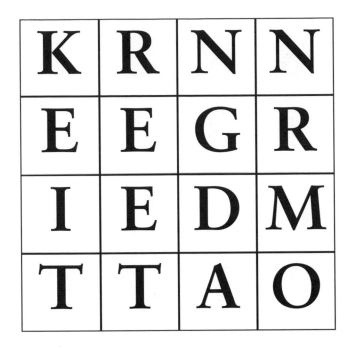

K	R	N	N
E	E	G	R
I	E	D	M
T	T	A	O

Puzzle 62
topics:
human quality,
leader,
employment

M	I	D	A
M	S	K	S
N	I	B	U
Y	M	R	A

Puzzle 63
topics:
legend,
anatomy,
religion

N	G	L	E
M	A	O	I
R	C	O	U
L	G	I	C

Puzzle 64
topics:
astronomy,
creature,
foodstuff

N	J	N	A
Y	B	U	U
L	E	E	B
L	E	N	B

196

Puzzle 65
topics:
mineral,
anatomy,
action

P	W	P	E
X	O	Z	X
I	A	R	N
E	A	N	C

Puzzle 66
topics:
language,
plant,
mineral

T	O	R	U
R	I	H	D
C	I	R	D
U	E	U	L

Puzzle 67
topics:
action,
tendency

A	T	B	B
R	E	H	I
O	A	I	T
L	E	T	S

Puzzle 68
topic:
quality

B	A	R	D
E	A	L	G
T	O	I	I
D	Y	B	I

Splits

These involve dividing a grid of symbols, each of which is assigned a value, into sections with similar totals. Sometimes the value of the symbols is known, other times the section borders are known. You will need to find the missing information.

Puzzle 69

Using three straight lines, split the grid into 6 subgroups so that the sum of symbols in each has a value of 16.

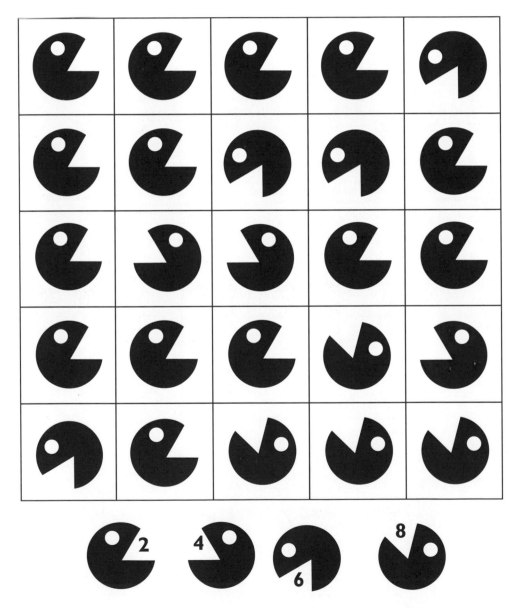

Puzzle 70

Using two straight lines, split the grid into four subgroups so that the sum of symbols in each has a value of 22.

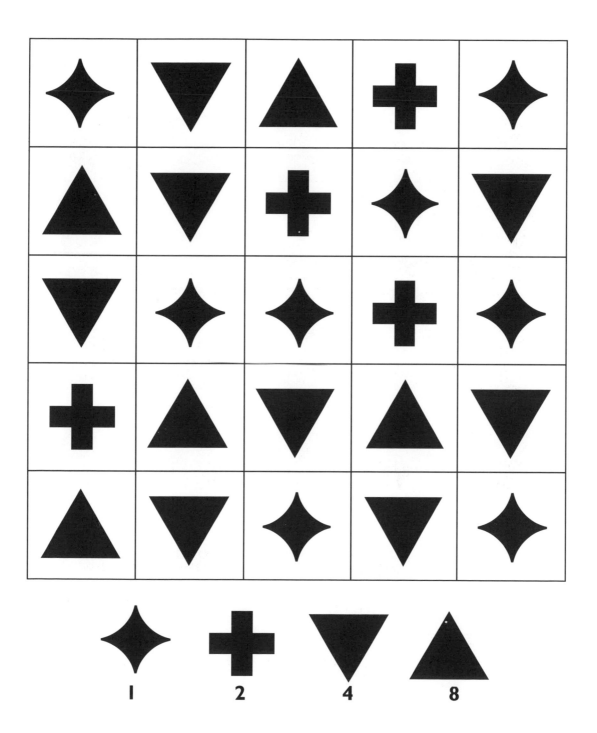

200

Each spiral is of a particular value. Which type of spiral should fill the empty squares so that the total value of each subgroup is 25?

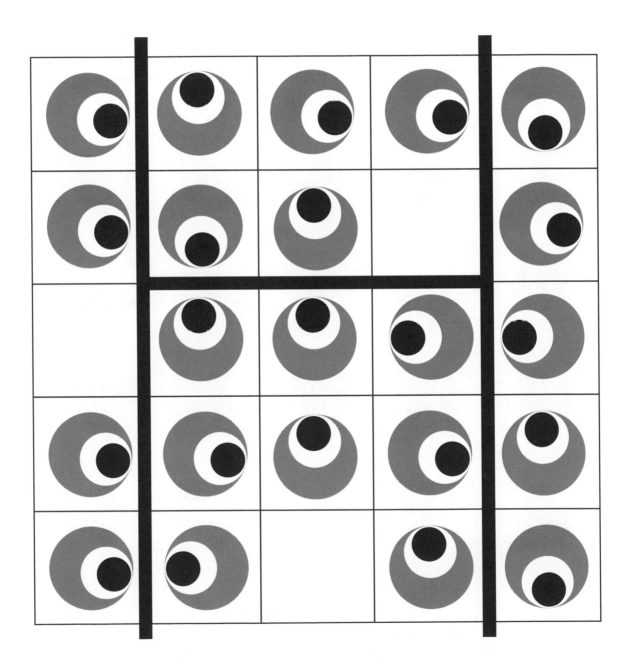

Puzzle 72

Each patterned square is of a particular value. Which pattern should fill all the empty squares so that the total value of each subgroup is 32?

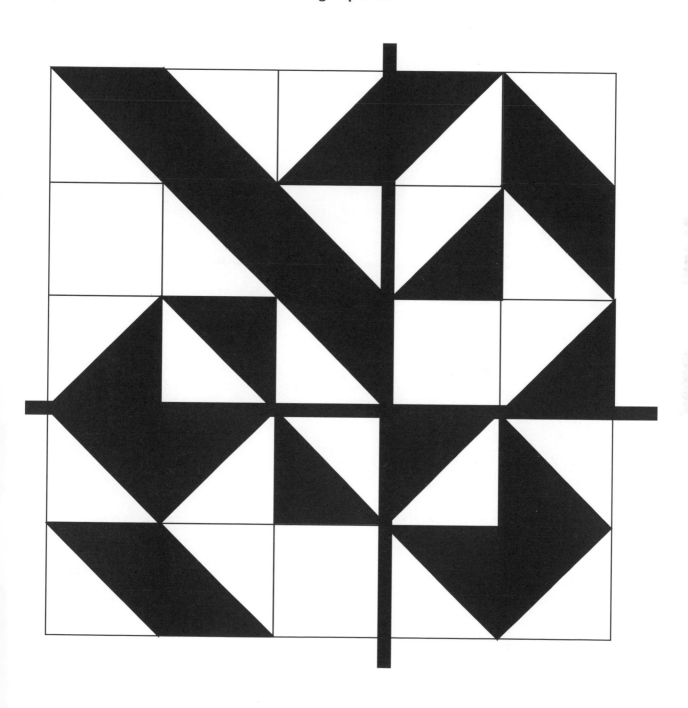

Puzzle 73

With the grid split as shown, what are the values of each fish, when the sum of each subgroup is 36?

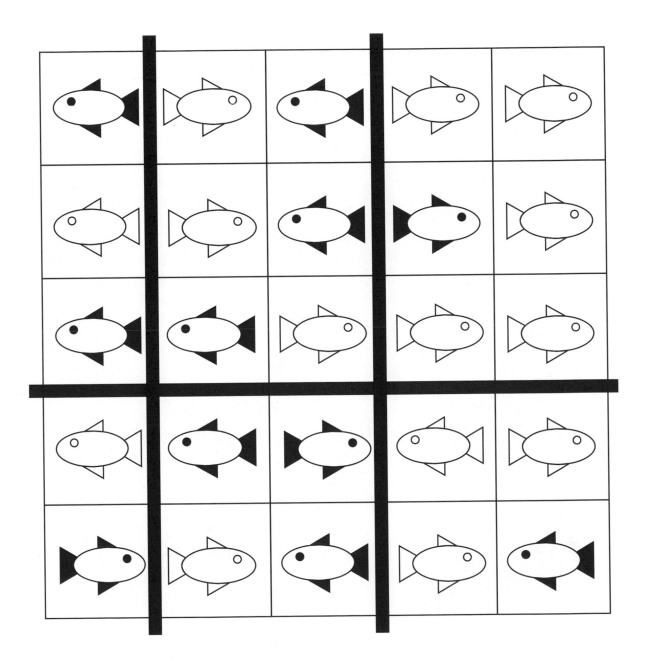

Puzzle 74

With the grid split as shown, what are the values of each suit when the sum of each subgroup is 21?

Killer stars

Many years ago Mensa, together with the London Times newspaper, used to run a competition called 'The Times Tournament of the Mind'. There were a number of rounds of increasingly mind-bending questions. Only the strong survived. However, though many of the contestants were formidably bright, there could be only one winner. Mensa's puzzle masters, Harold Gale and Robert Allen, came up with the idea of the Killer Question. It was usually in the form of a series which the contestants had to complete. No subject was too arcane to be turned into one of these series. For example, one of them required a knowledge of Canadian Prime Ministers since WW2 - not the sort of thing that even your average Canadian might be able to reel off on the spur of the moment. And bear in mind that there was no clue as to what the subject of the series was.

This section continues in that fine old tradition. The letters around the stars are the first letters of a conceptually linked series of words. They might refer to anything. The answer might be a single letter, but it might not. If you get even a couple of these right you should be hugely pleased with yourself. Don't get too obsessed. At least one former contestant spent so much work time trying to solve problems like these that he got the sack. You have been warned!

Puzzle 75

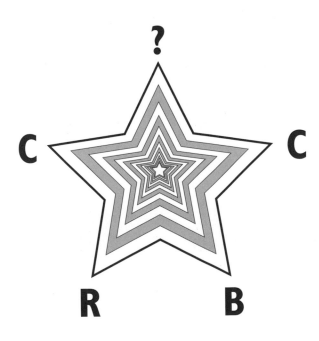

Puzzle 76

205

Puzzle 77

Puzzle 78

Puzzle 79

Puzzle 80

206

Puzzle 81

L ? Y

H Y

Puzzle 82

S ? W

H W

Puzzle 83

Puzzle 84

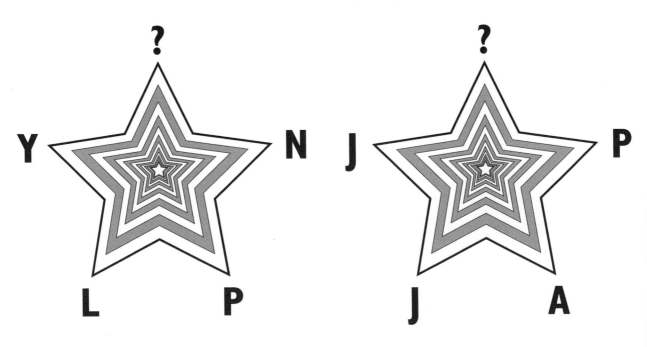

Y ? N

L P

J ? P

J A

Puzzle 85

Puzzle 86

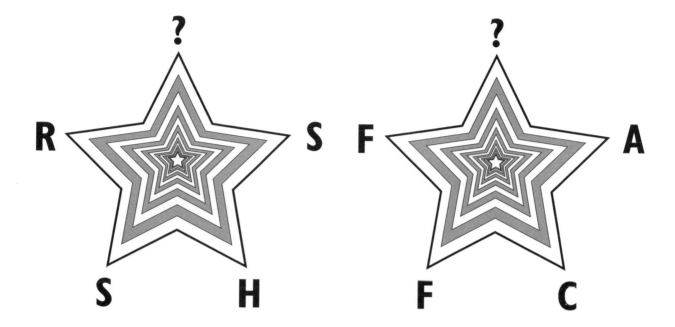

R   ?   S

S   H

F   ?   A

F   C

Advanced Word Searches

Even the humble wordsearch, that mainstay of coffee breaks throughout the world, can be turned into a genius puzzle. Those that follow are wordsearches, but not as you know them. For a start, the words are often not the sort you would use in everyday conversation. When was the last time 'Busuuti' passed your lips? Thought so. However, that is the least of your worries. In the searches that follow the words are not only spelled in any direction (that includes backwards), but they don't go in a straight line. Some have one bend, others have two, or even double back on themselves. Some of the words use the same letters over and over and guess what we filled the gaps with? Yep, the same letters. Evil, or what?

Puzzle 87

X	E	T	E	L	P	E	D	T	S	E	D	S	B	V
V	T	R	A	N	S	K	V	O	C	P	I	U	X	I
D	L	A	N	R	C	L	M	N	A	U	T	I	O	N
M	B	M	R	F	R	D	X	T	L	R	S	G	A	C
S	T	V	U	T	I	E	E	M	O	M	E	L	O	G
U	T	R	I	S	B	G	V	A	L	U	A	O	T	V
X	S	R	R	M	E	D	N	P	Q	U	V	E	X	A
J	E	S	A	B	R	I	R	B	C	F	G	I	P	T
E	T	G	Q	T	L	B	E	S	L	U	V	N	O	C
J	E	L	R	S	E	I	N	G	U	N	E	A	O	H
U	G	O	A	T	B	G	D	J	I	K	L	N	M	T
N	A	P	T	V	X	U	I	A	B	D	V	C	F	N
E	T	R	M	O	S	P	T	C	A	E	U	E	I	I
P	L	A	U	S	I	B	L	E	X	B	C	D	A	L
X	T	R	S	U	E	M	I	L	B	U	S	P	S	P

TRANSCRIBE   PLAUSIBLE   ABRIDGED   GOLEM
SEDITION   CONVEX   SUBLIME   DEPLETE
CONVULSE   VOCAL   GLOAT   TAGETES
STRATEGIC   JEJUNE   PLINTH

209

Puzzle 88

R	E	D	F	X	S	V	O	U	R	N	O	E	A	I
X	E	V	E	L	E	R	I	A	O	R	M	N	T	H
E	I	B	U	I	U	Q	U	T	S	U	P	V	M	C
L	Q	G	A	O	V	V	L	E	H	A	D	L	A	Y
L	E	R	U	R	L	I	A	X	A	P	E	T	T	E
T	S	T	P	S	B	G	E	X	G	E	V	Q	L	G
A	L	S	R	G	N	A	D	P	S	N	T	S	O	P
I	P	I	P	E	S	M	T	U	Y	I	V	T	D	T
P	P	F	T	U	M	L	S	I	D	C	O	B	I	O
B	U	S	T	N	S	N	T	Q	V	S	C	A	L	I
R	H	U	Q	L	T	A	R	X	T	E	L	C	H	C
S	G	U	T	I	R	E	E	V	A	T	E	T	A	T
B	T	J	P	M	U	I	N	I	H	P	L	E	D	U
O	U	K	L	P	D	D	Y	S	T	G	M	F	G	M
E	U	Q	I	P	E	A	I	X	A	N	I	N	O	R

REBARBATIVE
EXHUME
DELPHINIUM
BUSUUTI

LAYETTE
POSTVOCALIC
SERIATE
SEPTUM

DYSTAXIA
PIPISTRELLE
PIQUE
DYSGENIC

FLUVIAL
RONIN
MUTATE

Puzzle 89

R	N	A	L	H	E	L	A	L	I	H	P	O	S	V
E	S	E	O	U	G	I	O	P	T	Y	N	T	O	A
B	M	L	G	I	R	U	I	L	I	E	N	H	R	N
I	M	O	O	M	U	D	L	A	D	E	G	I	D	Y
H	N	P	O	T	O	R	G	C	T	B	Y	Z	E	G
P	R	O	G	E	B	O	O	I	E	J	V	I	N	O
T	A	K	N	R	U	S	R	R	N	D	E	C	R	L
E	L	E	O	N	A	O	B	N	A	E	A	A	E	O
R	E	T	I	O	F	P	M	S	L	L	P	R	T	D
C	P	G	N	C	M	H	I	A	S	P	S	T	S	E
N	R	K	S	U	U	O	T	T	P	I	G	S	O	A
O	S	U	I	H	L	L	S	E	O	O	P	O	P	P
C	M	L	I	Y	P	O	A	G	S	T	E	S	A	T
T	E	O	T	J	G	O	O	R	R	N	X	D	N	O
H	V	A	S	P	X	I	L	E	H	H	E	L	I	I

MUSCULAR	FAUBOURG	DROSOPHILA	GOOGOL
PENITENT	INSPISSATE	OSTRACIZE	POSTERN
MOPOKE	PAEDOLOGY	CONCRETION	HIBERNAL
HELIX	IMBROGLIO	HELIUM	GYVE

Puzzle 90

U	N	L	Y	L	E	M	I	T	U	N	H	D	L	C
I	U	M	B	R	A	D	A	N	J	N	A	T	U	I
M	T	U	D	E	U	N	E	U	U	E	I	N	B	T
I	N	E	U	S	V	V	D	U	R	V	C	U	N	I
W	U	D	N	R	O	O	E	N	T	I	K	V	U	R
I	N	E	G	O	L	S	L	O	N	G	N	A	N	A
N	H	R	O	H	P	L	E	R	U	J	L	A	C	G
D	O	A	D	N	U	A	N	E	R	U	U	N	T	U
U	L	R	L	U	N	V	A	T	O	H	L	R	R	E
N	U	T	L	E	O	A	N	T	S	A	M	E	D	B
V	N	L	I	E	E	E	U	A	S	L	N	E	M	A
O	T	U	H	F	S	H	P	N	T	B	O	A	M	A
L	O	P	G	R	U	P	S	L	A	S	P	H	N	L
D	U	U	N	L	O	U	T	P	A	R	S	L	P	P
U	N	E	A	L	R	E	C	L	U	R	Y	T	O	U

UMBRA   UGARITIC   UNHORSE   UNTIMELY
UNANELED   ULCEROUS   UNTREAD   UNWIND
UNARY   ULEMA   UPHILL   UPHEAVAL
ULTRARED   UNCINATE   UPHOLSTER

Puzzle 91

A	M	I	T	E	S	H	R	O	U	B	A	R	H	S
L	D	S	H	I	S	H	L	O	B	R	S	O	D	O
U	U	S	H	N	H	O	N	E	C	H	H	V	M	S
H	O	A	E	T	A	H	S	H	R	G	N	E	H	H
S	R	L	S	O	M	S	E	V	O	A	P	T	C	R
I	H	A	H	I	P	O	A	R	T	L	L	I	I	U
S	H	S	H	O	M	H	S	H	R	E	E	D	V	H
S	H	O	L	G	P	S	H	P	S	L	G	E	O	S
R	A	B	M	U	S	A	S	H	I	L	A	L	K	U
U	L	V	O	N	S	H	R	O	G	K	D	A	H	T
B	B	E	R	Y	S	U	O	D	N	E	T	S	T	M
U	P	L	O	R	H	M	N	I	S	S	N	U	G	T
R	S	L	E	K	E	N	R	A	O	N	S	E	U	O
H	H	S	V	T	R	H	V	H	P	O	T	L	V	H
S	L	M	R	U	S	T	S	S	H	U	T	T	R	S

SHINTO	SHOGUN	SHRUBBERY	SHROVE
SHILLELAGH	SHOSHONE	SHULAMITE	SHROUD
SHEKEL	SHOTGUN	SHRINKAGE	SHUSH
SHOSTAKOVICH	SHROVETIDE	SHUTTLE	

Puzzle 92

E	T	N	I	O	E	E	T	A	T	S	E	T	N	I
R	A	U	R	S	A	I	E	S	L	E	I	N	F	U
G	T	V	L	T	L	P	S	A	L	A	M	L	N	S
L	C	O	R	E	N	U	R	P	S	Z	D	L	O	I
A	C	I	A	L	M	O	F	U	A	E	B	A	D	M
B	L	V	Q	O	I	A	M	N	S	S	T	B	O	V
P	R	O	A	S	R	T	U	V	I	L	R	L	O	O
R	O	P	B	E	R	T	N	E	N	A	A	L	L	G
E	N	O	R	T	I	O	N	S	O	P	O	R	P	N
R	O	B	E	R	T	V	A	L	E	R	I	T	R	I
A	L	L	E	N	A	V	O	H	N	P	L	A	N	M
R	W	A	S	L	D	M	N	N	R	N	R	E	T	A
O	H	E	S	L	B	I	N	S	I	X	Y	O	R	L
U	R	E	A	D	O	R	O	T	V	C	A	B	L	F
G	N	A	L	S	T	U	I	T	A	N	O	T	N	I

ULEMA	PROPONENT	INTERGLACIAL	INFULAE
SLAVONIC	PROPORTIONAL	FLAMINGO	INHERIT
SLALOM	INTONATION	LANGUOR	INFUSION
SLEAZEBALL	INTESTATE	LANTERN	

Puzzle 93

M	T	I	I	T	A	U	M	E	E	R	M	E	D	I
O	O	S	M	D	O	D	I	O	T	S	E	C	O	T
U	P	E	E	R	E	D	P	D	P	R	U	S	M	A
L	D	D	M	P	U	E	L	E	T	E	O	E	P	T
L	U	C	E	S	M	A	S	C	A	R	I	C	E	D
A	D	R	T	I	T	D	T	E	R	P	U	I	T	E
T	O	M	E	D	E	S	I	L	U	M	D	T	A	C
S	O	R	E	E	D	U	D	E	T	R	O	M	I	T
P	R	S	I	T	P	P	E	R	A	O	S	R	E	S
E	D	O	M	E	T	R	L	A	T	I	S	D	E	Z
E	C	O	M	O	E	I	C	T	E	S	P	R	E	I
C	P	U	P	R	C	I	A	D	T	A	C	E	S	R
M	O	T	M	R	E	T	I	E	E	D	I	L	E	T
L	R	E	S	E	E	A	C	M	A	S	T	T	C	U
E	G	I	B	D	E	T	L	U	A	D	E	O	M	P

DESIDERATUM   DISTEMPERED   DOMESTICATED   PRESELECTED
COMPUTERIZE   DEMODULATOR   DEMASTICATED   RETICULATED
DECELERATES   COMPROMISED   AUDIOMETERS   COMPUTERIZED
DELETERIOUS   COMPETITORS   DUPLICATORS   PREMEDITATED
DEPRECIATED   MOULD-DEPOSIT   MASTERPIECE   SPEEDOMETER

Puzzle 94

T	R	P	A	S	F	T	R	E	U	A	P	H	A	I
H	O	L	O	E	O	R	U	A	L	S	R	E	O	F
E	O	C	O	R	A	O	T	S	S	G	E	T	B	O
C	A	T	R	E	H	S	E	E	T	E	J	A	M	R
O	S	M	R	C	A	S	R	E	G	A	B	A	O	E
L	T	U	A	E	Y	U	H	R	O	F	T	P	H	L
O	A	C	N	N	A	C	E	O	R	O	C	I	E	D
R	S	H	E	F	L	G	U	U	L	R	L	K	R	O
M	R	D	A	T	R	S	S	N	T	E	B	A	D	V
E	G	U	L	O	V	C	R	O	S	S	R	O	E	S
N	S	R	L	S	L	A	U	G	H	T	A	L	L	G
S	Y	E	C	H	R	S	R	O	A	E	D	O	L	E
E	E	B	R	A	E	R	R	T	K	R	E	C	A	T
D	C	R	R	A	E	S	E	S	T	E	S	G	E	H
R	E	L	A	E	L	L	O	C	A	D	Y	L	L	E

TREACHEROUS DECOLLETAGE REGULATORS HERETOFORE
STOREHOUSE OCTAHEDRAL CHARTREUSE COLORATURA
FORESTALLS SURROGATES REDECLARES SCHEDULERS
SLAUGHTERED RESEARCHERS REALLOCATES CROSSROADS
FORECASTERS FLAGEOLET ORTHOCLASE

GENIUS GYM ANSWERS

1. Opera, Books, Music, Paint, Poems.

2. Basic, Proud, Scrap, Price, Clasp.

3. Plague, Passed, Create, Fungus, Growth.

4. Prince, Cobble, Turret, Darken, Plunge, nonsense letters AKLPJN.

5. In all these puzzles assume that each triangle is labelled ABC starting at the apex and working clockwise. The answer to this puzzle is therefore A+B+C = 14.

6. (A x C) - B = 12.

7. Work it out as A + B + C, but then put the answer in the next triangle to your right. When you reach the end of the row, put the next answer in the first triangle. This time the answer is 16.

8. The answer is that we have no longer treated the triangles as separate entities but have used them as a group. To work out the answer add A + A + A and put the sum in the first triangle, B + B + B and put the sum in the second triangle and C + C + C will give you 9.

9. You should be able to work out that the letters represent numbers based on their positions in the alphabet (A=1, B= 2, etc). The formula is then (A x 2) + (B + C) and the answer is V.

10. This time the formula is (A + B) / C and the answer is B.

11. The alphabet is now numbered backwards (A=26, B=25, etc). The formula is A + B - C and so the answer is M.

12. (A x 2) + (B x 2) - C = 28.

13. This is not a calculation at all. The answer is that the name Mark Twain is spelt out around the triangles. The N is missing.

14. The word Einstein is spelt out around the triangles. So what is the missing letter? A for Albert.

15. 11. Add the outside numbers in each segment together and put their sum on the centre of the opposite segment.

16. 8. Add the outside numbers in each segment and put their sum in the centre of that segment.

17. 14. Multiply the outer numbers for each segment and put them in the centre of the next segment clockwise.

18. 10. Add the outer numbers and place their sum in the next-but-one segment clockwise.

19. 12. In each segment subtract the smaller outer number from the larger one. Double the difference and place it in the centre of the segment two places anti-clockwise.

20. 6. Add all the outer digits in each segment together and place the sum in the centre.

21. The sequence is ACDB and works left to right across the matrix.

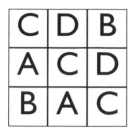

C	D	B
A	C	D
B	A	C

22. The sequence is 1432 and works in a horizontal bustrophedon. A bustrophedon is the 'ox plough' pattern which goes from one side to the other, turns round and comes back again.

3	4	1
4	3	2
1	2	3

23. The sequence is FXALP and works in a diagonal bustrophedon starting at the top left.

P	F	F
X	P	A
L	L	L

24. The sequence is ZTABX and works in an inward spiral starting at the top left.

B	X	B
B	Z	X
X	T	Z

25. The sequence is VABCTUVP and works in a diagonal bustrophedon which starts at the top left.

C	P	V
V	P	A
V	B	P

26. The sequence is 324659 and runs in an anticlockwise helix starting at the bottom right.

5	2	4
9	4	6
3	6	5

27. The men are monks. The brothers have been newly posted by their Order to a monastery they have never been to before. The 'father' is the Abbot.

28. These kittens are young rabbits, not young cats.

29. Grandpa was on a life-support machine. As it happened the clock was on the same circuit. At 12.13am there was a power cut and both stopped. Before the emergency generator could kick in, grandpa was dead.

30. Charlie threw a snow ball.

After it broke the glass, it lay in pieces on the carpet. Before her parents came home the central heating came on and first melted the scattered snow and then dried up the damp patch.

31. The driver had jumped out of the car when he lost control at the top of the hill. His fall accounts for the cuts and bruises. He got back inside in order to get his briefcase.

32. A serial. Each sentence contains an anagram of the country mentioned.

33. Joe was an undertaker by profession. The caller had wanted him to bring the funeral bier.

34. Holes.

35. Becky's family are Jewish. They would have been in the synagogue the day before the accident, the Jewish Sabbath. The injured were all passers-by.

36. Pizzazz.

37. I. Nine forwards.

218

38. N. Three forwards, one back.

39. J. Miss 4 each time.

40. O. Miss two each time.

41. S. Miss three each time.

42. E. If you look carefully you'll see that the letters spell out W. Shakespeare.

43. C. The sequence is of Roman numerals I V X L C D M.

44. 13. $(A^2 + D) - (B + C)$.

45. 10. $(A^2 + C^2) - (D^2 + B^2)$.

46. 16. A+A+A+A, B+B+B+B, etc.

47. 34. $(A + D) + (B2 - C)$.

48. 33. A + B + C + D. Square 1 goes to Square 3, Square 3 goes to Square 1. Square 2 goes to Square 4, Square 4 goes to Square 2.

49. 23. $(A \times C) - (B + D)$.

50. 42. $A^2 - B + C2 - D$. Square 1 goes to 4, Square 4 goes to 1. Square 2 goes to 3, Square 3 goes to 2.

51. 20. $(A + B + C - D) \times 2$.

52.

53.

54.

55. They are the initials of the months, plus initials of the seasons.

56. They are the initials of the planets plus the words Sun and Moon.

57. Stanza, Verse, Rhyme

58. Alkaline, Composer

59. Bezel, Jejune, Grace.

60. Piquet, Lustrum, Gnu.

61. Marketed, Nitrogen

62. Misandry, Imam, Busk

63. Golem, Iconic, Gular.

64. Nebula, Blenny, Jube.

65. Zircon, Paxwax, Open.

66. Urdu, Rutile, Orchid.

67. Obliterate, Habits

68. Biodegradability.

69.

70.

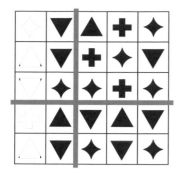

71. The symbol worth 5 below.

| I | 5 | 3 | 8 |

72. The symbol worth 4 below.

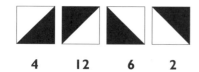

| 4 | 12 | 6 | 2 |

73.

| 4 | 16 | 8 | 20 |

74.

| 3 | 4 | 7 | I |

75. N (Nixon). These are all US Presidents working backwards from Clinton. The series goes: Clinton, Bush, Reagan, Carter, Nixon.

76. A (Andropov). These are Soviet leaders starting with Lenin. The series is: Lenin, Stalin, Kruschev, Brezhnev, Andropov.

77. NI (Northern Ireland). These are the countries of Great Britain and Ireland. The series goes: Scotland, England, Wales, Eire, Northern Ireland. If you got U for Ulster you can count it as a correct answer even though Ulster and Northern Ireland are not strictly the same.

78. ND (North Dakota). These are the first five US states that have a border with Canada. West to east they go: Washington, Idaho, Montana, North Dakota, Minnesota.

79. I (Friday). These are the third letters of days of the week: MoNday, TuEsday, WeDnesday, ThUrsday, FrIday.

80. G (gigabyte). These are the units of data used in computing. They are in ascending order of size: bit, byte, kilobyte, megabyte, gigabyte.

81. Y (May). Last letters of the months: JanuarY, FebruarY, MarcH, ApriL, MaY.

82. H (Henry II). These are the first five kings of England: William I, William II, Henry I, Stephen, Henry II.

83. T (Tudor). These are the royal houses of England in chronological order: Norman, Plantagenet, Lancaster, York, Tudor.

84. P (Philip). These are the first disciples of Jesus: Peter, Andrew, James, John, Philip.

85. Y (Mercury). Last letters of the planets leading outwards from the sun: MercurY, VenuS, EartH, MarS, JupiteR.

86. If you got this right without cheating, you probably are a genius. The answer is H (Humboldtianum). They are the seas of the Moon in alphabetical order: Australe, Crisium, Fecunditatis, Frigoris, Humboldtianum.

87.

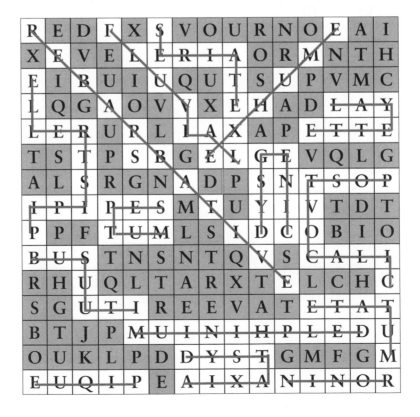

```
X E T E L P E D T S E D S B V
V T R A N S K V O C P I U X I
D L A N R C L M N A U T I O N
M B M R F R D X T L R S G A C
S T V U T I E E M O M E L O G
U T R I S B G V A L U A O T V
X S P R M E D N P Q U V E X A
J E S A B R I R B C F G I P T
E T G Q T L B E S L U V N O C
J E L R S E I N G U N E A O H
U G O A T B G D J I K L N M T
N A P T V X U I A B D U C F N
E T R M O S P T C A E U E I I
P L A U S I B L E X B C D A L
X T R S U E M I L B U S P S P
```

88.

```
R E D F X S V O U R N O E A I
X E V E L E R I A O R M N T H
E I B U I U Q U T S U P V M C
L Q G A O V Y X E H A D L A Y
L E R U P L L A X A P E T T E
T S T P S B G E L G L V Q L G
A L S R G N A D P S N T S O P
I P I P E S M T U Y I V T D T
P P F T U M L S I D C O B I O
B U S T N S N T Q V S C A L I
R H U Q L T A R X T E L C H C
S G U T I R E E V A T E T A T
B T J P M U I N I H P L E D U
O U K L P D D Y S T G M F G M
E U Q I P E A I X A N I N O R
```

89.

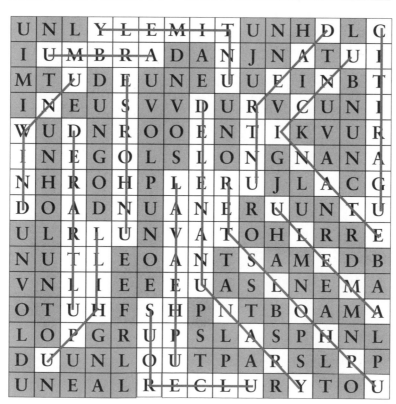

90.

91.

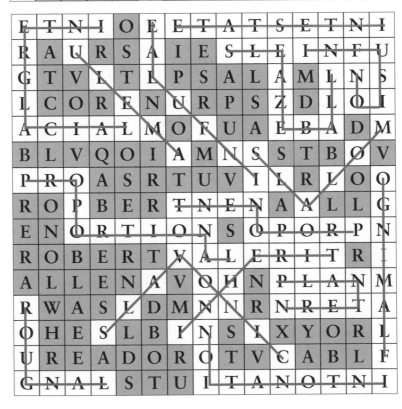

A	M	I	T	E	S	H	R	O	U	B	A	R	H	S
L	D	S	H	I	S	H	L	O	B	R	S	O	D	O
U	U	S	H	N	H	O	N	E	C	H	H	V	M	S
H	O	A	E	T	A	H	S	H	R	G	N	E	H	H
S	R	L	S	O	M	S	E	V	O	A	P	T	C	R
I	H	A	H	I	P	O	A	R	T	L	L	I	I	U
S	H	S	H	O	M	H	S	H	R	E	E	D	V	H
S	H	O	L	G	P	S	H	P	S	L	G	E	O	S
R	A	B	M	U	S	A	S	H	I	L	A	L	K	U
U	L	V	O	N	S	H	R	O	G	K	D	A	H	T
P	B	E	R	Y	S	U	O	D	N	E	T	S	T	M
U	P	L	O	R	H	M	N	I	S	S	N	U	G	T
R	S	L	E	K	E	N	R	A	O	N	S	E	U	O
H	H	S	V	T	R	H	V	H	P	O	T	L	V	H
S	L	M	R	U	S	T	S	S	H	U	T	T	R	S

92.

E	T	N	I	O	E	E	T	A	T	S	E	T	N	I
R	A	U	R	S	A	I	E	S	L	E	I	N	F	U
G	T	V	L	T	L	P	S	A	L	A	M	L	N	S
L	C	O	R	E	N	U	R	P	S	Z	D	L	O	I
A	C	I	A	L	M	O	F	U	A	E	B	A	D	M
B	L	V	Q	O	I	A	M	N	S	S	T	B	O	V
P	R	O	A	S	R	T	U	V	I	L	R	L	O	O
R	O	P	B	E	R	T	N	E	N	A	A	L	L	G
E	N	O	R	T	I	O	N	S	O	P	O	R	P	N
R	O	B	E	R	T	V	A	L	E	R	I	T	R	I
A	L	L	E	N	A	V	O	H	N	P	L	A	N	M
R	W	A	S	L	D	M	N	N	R	N	R	E	T	A
O	H	E	S	L	B	I	N	S	I	X	Y	O	R	L
U	R	E	A	D	O	R	O	T	V	C	A	B	L	F
G	N	A	L	S	T	U	L	T	A	N	O	T	N	I

93.

94.

FINAL THOUGHT

Now you've read what I have to say about genius, and have consulted your friends and thought about the subject yourself, go back and reconsider the list you wrote before you had read anything about the subject. What does your new list look like? Is it the same as the old one or different? If there are some that were not in the first list, why are they included now? If anyone has been removed from the first list, why was that?

Name   **Claim to genius**   **Reason for inclusion in list**